Women AND WORK IN AMERICA

Women AND WORK IN AMERICA

By ROBERT W. SMUTS

SCHOCKEN BOOKS • NEW YORK

Introduction to the
Paperback Edition

SLIGHTLY more than a decade has passed since the publication of Robert W. Smuts's study of *Women and Work in America*. It is both necessary and desirable that this paperback edition carry a new preface. It is necessary so that the reader can learn about the transformations in the role of women in the labor market that have occurred since the late 1950's; it is desirable so that attention can be called to some of the research that has been carried out since then by the Conservation of Human Resources Project at Columbia University to which Robert Smuts was attached when he wrote his book, as well as to investigations carried out by others.

In 1966 and 1967 the Conservation Project published *Life Styles of Educated Women*, by Eli Ginzberg *et al.*, and *Educated American Women: Self Portraits*, by Ginzberg and Yohalem, Columbia University Press. The bibliography in the former volume calls attention to the major studies that appeared in the years following the appearance of Smuts's work.

The most readily accessible up-to-date bibliography on women and work is that in the *1969 Handbook on Women Workers* (U.S. Department of Labor, Women's Bureau Bulletin 294). This Bulletin also provides the best organized and most authoritative body of factual data about women and work. Three additional recent studies will enable the interested reader to become broadly acquainted with the subject: Helen S. Astin, *The Woman Doctorate in America* (Russell Sage Foundation, 1969), Cynthia F. Epstein, *Woman's Place* (University of California, 1970), and John R. Shea and Associates, *Dual Careers* (The Ohio State University, Center for Human Resources Research, Volume One, May 1970).

Let us first examine the principal continuities and changes that have occurred in the role of women in work since Smuts looked at the scene in the late 1950's. Despite the passage of more than a decade, little change has occurred in the following areas. Women remain heavily concentrated in a relatively few occupations and industries: in the service fields, in clerical and sales positions, as operatives in manufacturing, and within the professions of teaching, nursing, and social work.

Moreover, only a minority of all women, about two out of five, work full-time, full-year. When we compare the earnings of those who work full-time, full-year with the earnings of men, we see that women continue to earn much less than men; in 1968 they averaged $4,500, or only 58 percent of the average of $7,700 earned by men. Smuts stated that women earned two-thirds as much as men; the intervening period has actually witnessed a worsening in their relative earning position.

Smuts pointed out that women were conspicuously underrepresented among workers who earned $10,000 or more. This is still true: in 1968 only 3 percent of all full-time women workers earned above that figure, while the comparable figure for men was 28 percent. However, the proportion of women among full-time workers with high incomes increased in the 1960's.

Working wives continue to help their families to enjoy a middle-class standard of living: they account for about one-quarter of total income for all families earning more than $7,000; among those in the $10,000 to $15,000 range, their average contribution is even higher, amounting to 28 percent of total family income.

Now let us look briefly at some of the important changes that have occurred since the mid-fifties, which was Smuts's cut-off point. In some instances the recent data represent a continuation of a trend that goes back to World War II or earlier. In 1955 there were 20 million women in the labor force; in 1968, there were more than 29.2 million. This increase was reflected in a substantial rise in the percentage of women among all workers—from 31 to 37 percent. In the mid-fifties, of all women sixteen years of age and over, slightly more than one in three was in the labor force; in 1968, more than two in five were in the labor force.

If we disregard the youngsters under eighteen and the oldsters over sixty-five, we find that in 1968 there were two age groups in which more than half of all the women were in the labor force: the group between twenty and twenty-four and those between forty-five and fifty-four. This finding underscores a new development—that women's attachment to work now is pervasive throughout the entire adult group, except for those over sixty-five years old, of whom only one in ten works. In 1968 just under one out of every two women over eighteen years of age was in the labor force, compared with two out of five a decade or so earlier.

As we might expect, the marital status of a woman and

particularly whether she has children, especially young children at home, have a direct influence on whether she is working or looking for work. In 1969, the following percentages of women were in the labor force according to their marital status: divorced, 72; married, husband absent, 54; single, 51; married, husband present, 40; widowed, 26. Of the 30 million women who were working or looking for work in 1969, 17.6 million, or almost three out of five, were married women living with their husbands.

Of the approximately 23.4 million women in the labor force in 1968 who were married or who had been married, 11.6 million, or almost half, had children under eighteen years of age. Since it is generally easier for a woman to work after her youngest child enters school, it should be noted that of the 11.6 million with children under eighteen, 7.4 million had children between the ages of six and seventeen. Of the remaining 4.2 million, half had children under the age of three, and half had children between the ages of three and six.

Slightly over two out of five women with children under eighteen were in the labor force, a slightly higher percentage than for women without children! However, the probability that a woman with children would work was reduced if her children were young. Of those with no children under six, 51 percent worked; of those with no children under three, 37 percent worked; of those with children under three, 25 percent worked.

The striking change that occurred between the mid-fifties and the end of the sixties is that the labor force participation of mothers increased from about one in four to two in five, which was a much more rapid rate of increase than for all women workers. Interestingly, this is true of mothers of both older and younger children. In fact the most rapid increase in labor force participation has occurred among mothers of children under six; this group showed a gain in labor market participation of over 60 percent during the past decade, with the result that now almost one-third of such mothers work.

The other trend worth noting relates to the impact of education on women's working. In general, the more education a woman has, the more likely she is to be in the labor force. For instance, among high school dropouts the participation rate is slightly under 40 percent; for college graduates, 54 percent; for women with five or more years of college, over 70 percent.

The following points about the present scene should be borne in mind when reading Smuts's book:

Women remain concentrated in a limited number of occupations and industries which are characterized by relatively low wage structures.

The gap between women's and men's earnings has been widening; women currently earn less than three-fifths as much as men.

Women now account for 37 percent of all workers; approximately one out of two adult women are in the labor force. Most women who work are married and most of these married women workers have children. About one out of three women with children under six are at work.

The more education a woman has, the more likely it is that she will be in the labor force. Among those who have gone beyond their baccalaureate, about seven out of ten have jobs or are looking for one.

These several interfaces between women and work were of concern to Smuts, and they continue to concern students of the early 1970's. But in the intervening decade five new dimensions have surfaced that were muted or ignored by earlier investigators, including Smuts. To these we now turn for a brief consideration.

As part of the surfacing of interest in the poor and in programs aimed at the reduction of poverty, attention has recently been focused on women heads-of-households who work but whose earnings are insufficient to enable them to lift themselves and their dependents out of poverty. In 1968, there were approximately 5.4 million families headed by females. Of this number, 3.2 million female heads-of-household, or approximately three out of five, worked during the course of the year. Of those who worked, almost half worked full-time. There were three white families to one Negro family in America, which underscores the disproportionate number of Negro households in which a woman was the head, since the number of these Negro families was about three times more than would have been expected without special factors.

Of the 5.4 million families headed by females, 1.7 million, or just under one in three, were living in poverty. One-fourth of the white families were living in poverty, in contrast to one-half of the Negro families. Slightly less than one of two female heads of these poverty-stricken families worked. Over 200,000 out of 700,000, or roughly 30 percent, of those who worked full-time were unable to earn enough to raise their families above the poverty line. Of the families with female heads who worked year-round full-time, Negroes were four times more likely than whites to be caught in poverty!

This becomes more understandable when one notes that many Negro women were employed as private household workers. In this occupation, year-round, full-time women workers averaged only $1,500; in other types of service work, the average earnings for women came to only $3,300.

In 1967 the Congress amended the Social Security Act in the hope of encouraging many women heads-of-households who were receiving Aid for Dependent Children (AFDC) to seek training and employment rather than to look to their welfare checks as their sole source of support. The amendments permitted welfare recipients in training or in a job to retain a part of their earnings. President Nixon's Family Assistance Plan of 1970 is predicated on building in a broad work incentive for persons on welfare in the hope and expectation that it will serve as a bridge to help them return to regular employment and self-supporting status.

The concern of the Congress and the public with rising welfare costs is centered on the AFDC program, through which 4.9 million children in 1.7 million families, a total of 6.6 million persons, received assistance in 1969. And the case load continued to rise at the rate of 17 percent over the preceding twelve months. Since the program costs $3 billion annually—up from $1 billion in 1960—the determination of the Administration to explore new approaches is readily understandable.

But the efforts of the Work Incentive Program and the new Family Assistance Plan to encourage female heads-of-household who are receiving AFDC to accept training and employment will encounter resistance, particularly from mothers with pre-school children. Although the Congress has belatedly decided to appropriate sizable sums to build and operate child-care facilities, the shortage of these facilities is acute. There are only 400,000 licensed places, and the costs average in excess of $1,000 per child per year, running up to and over $2,500 in New York City!

Although many mothers who receive AFDC do not have pre-school children to care for, their potential to become fully self-supporting is limited because of their lack of skill, the low wages that they can earn, and the sizable costs connected with employment: clothing, transportation, meals. This is not to say that the effort should not be made to offer such women opportunities to take training and help in finding employment, but this simple fact cannot be blinked: Many women without husbands are unable to support their families even if they hold down full-time jobs.

Another striking development of the 1960's that could not have been anticipated was the passage by the Congress of Title VII of the Civil Rights Act, which prohibits sex discrimination in employment. When Judge Smith of the Rules Committee expanded the bill to prohibit discrimination based on sex, he believed that he was giving the coup de grâce to a bill designed to outlaw discrimination based on race. He could not believe that his colleagues would consider giving broad federal protection to women by preventing their being discriminated against in the work arena. But Congress passed the Civil Rights Act with the provision on sex discrimination included.

The passage of this legislation has not yet had a major effect on the status of women in the labor market. It was not until the summer of 1970 that the government brought its first case to court. But the Equal Employment Opportunity Commission has devoted a considerable amount of its time and energy to cases involving discrimination based on sex and has had some success in getting employers to modify their employment policies and practices. For instance, it is no longer permissible for an airline to dismiss a hostess after a decade or so of satisfactory service simply on the ground that she has passed her high point in attractiveness. Moreover, the EEOC has opened jobs previously closed to women and has insisted on the elimination of unjustified wage differentials.

The existence of the legislation and the Commission have undoubtedly exerted pressure on many employers to take corrective action. Most large companies and even many smaller ones have made changes in their personnel policies to avoid getting into conflict with the law and to stay abreast of the times.

This brings us to the Women's Liberation Movement, which is the last of the new dimensions that we will briefly explore. It is not easy to define and describe Women's Lib, or to distill what is new about it; it is more difficult to calculate its long-term effect. In a country and a world in which a great many people, especially young people, are expressing their dissatisfactions with the status quo, it is hardly surprising that a rebellious, revolutionary stance has been adopted by small numbers of women who are dissatisfied with the manner in which society treats them.

Their complaints cover the gamut: they say that they are brought up to serve as sex objects; they are discouraged from developing their intellectual potential; they face major handicaps if they seek to pursue a career. Moreover, if they marry and have children, it is understood that if they work they must make all the compromises between family and job. Men, on the other hand, are supposed to keep their eyes on their careers; in fact, their wives are supposed to help them do so.

What do the leaders of the militant Women's Lib want? They would like the world to turn itself around so that all the barriers and difficulties that women now face in trying to live their lives as men are able to live theirs are removed. They want equality here and now—equality of opportunity and equality of rewards. The most measured analysis of what this policy implies is found in the report of the Swedish Government to the United Nations in 1968 on *The Status of Women in Sweden*, which included the following proposition:

> The division of functions between the sexes must be changed in such a way that both the man and the woman in a family are afforded the same practical opportunities of participating in both active parenthood and gainful employment. If women are to attain a position in society outside the home which corresponds to their proportionate membership of the citizen body, it follows that men must assume a greater share of the responsibility for the upbringing of children and the care of their home.

This may not be all that Women's Liberation has in mind, but it surely helps to fill out the specifics of their program. When the National Manpower Council in the mid-fifties was working on its study of *Womanpower* (Columbia, 1957), we used to say that there were few problems confronting women that could not be solved if one were willing to create a whole host of difficulties for men.

As we enter the 1970's, this is the broad picture. Women are in the labor force to stay. In the years ahead, an even higher proportion are likely to work. For those who are most interested in supplementing their husband's incomes, the job situation is favorable: there are a large number of white-collar and service jobs for which women workers are preferred, particularly if they want, as so many do, to work part-time or part-year.

The outlook is less favorable for women who are seriously interested in a career which they would like to combine with family and children. The labor market continues to be inflexible when it comes to part-time jobs for professional women and it continues to discriminate against women. But on the latter front, remedial action has been started and the years ahead should see more women making it to the top—or at least close to the top.

The acute worries about the impact of mothers' working on the well-being of their children have receded, but wide-scale social restiveness remains. American society is still ambivalent about whether it is sound public policy to encourage mothers to work by establishing more child-care facilities. But a decision has been made that this is desirable policy to help poor mothers work and to help industries which suffer from manpower shortages. It would seem therefore that the die has been cast and the years ahead will see a vast increase in child-care facilities.

The United States as well as other advanced economies such as England, Sweden, France, Germany, and Canada are far down the road where women will once again be closely involved—as they were in agricultural societies—in the production of goods and services. By the time all women who want to work have the opportunity to do so, these advanced economies will probably be faced with a new set of challenges about authority and responsibility in work, the balancing of work and leisure, and equity in the rewards from work. By that time the problems which inform Smuts's monograph and this Introduction will have been relegated, as they should be, to a place in the nation's historical development.

ELI GINZBERG

Columbia University
August, 1970

Foreword

Women and Work in America grows out of the research of the Conservation of Human Resources Project, which was established by General Eisenhower at Columbia University in 1950, and which included within its program historical studies of the nation's human resources.

With the passage of every year American social scientists are increasingly relying upon the use of elaborate statistical and mathematical methods and are selecting problems for investigation to which such methods are peculiarly well adapted. It is not necessary to denigrate these quantitative approaches to point out the danger of neglecting the contribution that can be made by imaginative historical inquiry. Mr. Smuts's study demonstrates, among other things, the value of the historian's approach in deepening our understanding of complex social developments.

A major revolution has occurred in the United States in the position of women in the world of work. This revolution was caused by, and in turn contributed to, major transformations in every sector of society—the home, the school, the work place, and the larger culture. It is not easy to disentangle the myriad forces that have helped to transform the face of the American economy in the twentieth century by adding millions of women to the work force. Statistics help to establish the scale of the revolution, but they cannot by themselves offer the illumination in depth which is required for understanding both what has happened and why.

The present volume derives its authenticity and interest in large measure from its reliance on contemporary sources. Mr. Smuts has sought to delineate the changing place of women in the world of work by drawing on these rich records and in good part by letting the women tell their own story.

In writing his book Mr. Smuts was influenced by several developments growing out of the large-scale researches at Columbia University into human resources and manpower problems. As the principal investigator for the Conservation of Human Resources Project studies entitled "The American Worker: 1890–1950," and as a member of the National Manpower Council staff during the two-year study that resulted in the publication of *Womanpower* (1957), Mr. Smuts had the opportunity to become well acquainted with the source materials bearing on the American worker since the turn of the century. In both instances he worked under the general supervision of Professor Henry David, who has had over-all responsibility for the research on the American worker and for shaping the Council's study of womanpower.

ELI GINZBERG
Director, Conservation of
Human Resources Project

Columbia University
December 4, 1958

Acknowledgments

AMONG the many who have helped in large ways and small to produce this book, I owe special thanks to Dr. Eli Ginzberg and Dr. Henry David for their valuable suggestions and guidance at every step, from first plans to final revision, and even more, for their contribution during years of close association to my understanding of the history of work in American society. I also wish to thank all of the members of the Conservation of Human Resources Project and of the National Manpower Council staff for ideas, facts, and critical judgment. Mr. Dale Hiestand was especially helpful. Dr. Gertrude Bancroft, Special Assistant for Manpower Statistics, U.S. Bureau of the Census, read and commented on the final manuscript. I am indebted to my wife, Alice Smuts, for helping to make the book more readable.

I am grateful to these publishers for permission to quote from the following works: Appleton-Century-Crofts, Inc., for *The Long Day*, by Dorothy Richardson; P. F. Collier & Son Corporation, for *Workers of the Nation*, by Gilson Willets; Doubleday & Company, Inc., for *The Woman Who Toils*, by Mrs. John Van Vorst and Marie Van Vorst; Houghton Mifflin Company, for *Earth Horizon: Autobiography*, by Mary Austin; G. P. Putnam's Sons, for *Once Upon a Time and Today*, by Maude Nathan; Routledge and Kegan Paul, Ltd., for *Old World Questions and New World Answers*, by Daniel Pidgeon.

ROBERT W. SMUTS

Contents

Women AND WORK IN AMERICA

Chapter I

THE WORK
OF WOMEN

HOUSEKEEPING is still the main occupation of American
women, but no longer the only occupation of most of them.
More than half of all women between the ages of eighteen
and fifty-five now spend at least part of each year working
for pay. In any one week, according to the reports of the
Census Bureau, the labor force now claims about 36 percent
of all the girls and women who have passed their fourteenth
birthdays. The new role of women in the labor force con-
stitutes a genuine revolution, not only in the lives of women,
but in the American economy and the American family as
well. Nearly every branch of the economy has become
irrevocably dependent upon the labors of the one worker
out of three who is a woman, and whether she realizes it or
not, today's schoolgirl is likely to spend half her adult years
in paid employment.

Revolutionary as these developments are, it would be
easy to overestimate their import. They do not, for instance,
represent the large-scale emergence of women from the
status of consumers to become, for the first time, productive
members of the economy. Women have always spent a
good deal of their time and energy meeting the purely

material wants of their families. The recent sharp increase in the number of women in paid employment is a revolution, not so much in the amount of work performed by women, or in the number of women who work, as in the kind of work they do.

The distinguishing feature of the work of women who are counted as members of the labor force is money: they are counted if they work for pay or profit.[1] Work, of course, may be defined in many ways, but it is common practice today, especially in economic studies, to define it as the Census does, and to ignore all other kinds of work. Even in common usage, we frequently deny the name work to any activity not aimed at making money.

However natural it may seem, this distinction is relatively new. During most of the nineteenth century, the United States was still predominantly rural and agricultural. For most people, work and the other activities of life were inextricably mingled. In the typical farm family everyone worked together, mainly to produce what the family consumed itself. Toward the end of the century, however, the United States was rapidly becoming a nation of cities, of commerce, and of industry. In the city, unlike the country, work was often distinct and separate from the rest of life. Some individuals left the home and the family for a definite part of each day and went to work to earn money. This change in the nature of work affected men and women very differently. From the beginning, some women followed work as it left the home, but most of those who went to work for wages and salaries were men. Most women, and nearly all married women, stayed home. Even when the family moved to the city, however, women continued to produce much of the food, clothing, and other necessities consumed by their families, and many of them took on paid work which they could perform without leaving home.

The proportion of women working for pay or profit has been increasing ever since the Civil War, if not before, but until World War II the change was relatively slow. As recently as 1940, six out of seven married women were full-time housewives, and it appeared that for most women paid work would continue to be no more than a brief episode in early life. Since the beginning of World War II, however, more and more women have been joining their husbands, brothers, and sons in the labor force. Today, nearly one third of all wives are combining housework with paid employment, and the proportion doing so is still increasing rapidly.

The shift from unpaid to paid employment is only one aspect of a continuing revolution in women's work. At least as significant has been the shift from paid work at home to paid work outside the home. Until late in the nineteenth century probably the majority of the women who earned money worked at home. Today, like most men, most of the women in the labor force work away from home. In spite of these changes, however, the home and the family remain at the center of women's lives, and the larger part of their enormous contribution to the wealth and welfare of the nation is still the work they perform inside the home and without pay. To interpret the changing work of American women it is essential, therefore, to consider how urban and industrial growth have affected their activities at home as well as their work in the labor force.

As the nineteenth century drew to a close, the United States still showed many of the marks of its pioneer past.

In 1890, the Census found that it could no longer draw a line between the settled and the unsettled portions of the West, and announced, therefore, that the frontier was closed. Yet, much of the West was as wild as ever. Billy the Kid and Jesse James were both shot in 1881, but it was not until ten years later that the Dalton Boys began their brief career of violence in the Oklahoma Territory. The sod hut had not yet disappeared from the prairies and plains, nor the log cabin from the river bottoms. Two thirds of the nation's population still lived in rural areas in 1890, and nearly half of its families still made their living from the soil.

At the same time, signs of twentieth-century America were everywhere. The electric trolley car had already ushered in the age of the commuter and suburban expansion. The cities were hard pressed to accommodate the hordes arriving each year from the farms and from abroad in search of opportunity. Between 1880 and 1890, New York City grew from a million to a million and a half people, and both Philadelphia and Chicago passed the million mark. The horseless carriage was still a curiosity, but the telephone, the electric light, and the typewriter were all in daily use. The huge network of railroads uniting the states of the East and West, the North and the South, was virtually complete. The Sherman Antitrust Act, passed in 1890, testified to the growing size and power of the corporation.

The conventions governing American women also showed much that was old and much that was new. Victorian notions of female delicacy and gentility, still current among the middle classes in the East, were passing out of fashion in the Midwest. Referring to her adolescence in a small town in Illinois in the mid-1880's, the author Mary Austin wrote that her set already . . . was beginning to spoof at the notion that, though a really nice girl could cross her ankles in company, she must not cross her knees, and at the notion, which Mary found active in some quarters as late as the early nineteen-hundreds, that a hatpin was a lascivious device invented for the purpose of allowing young women to show off their figures by raising their arms in the presence of young men.[2]

Under the common law, according to Blackstone,

the husband and the wife are one person . . . ; that is, the very being or legal existence of the woman is suspended during the marriage, or at least is incorporated . . . into that of her husband. . . . For this reason, a man cannot grant anything to his wife, or enter into covenant with her; for the grant would be to suppose her separate existence; and to covenant with her, would be only to covenant with himself. . . .[3]

This principle, though modified by statute and interpretation, had not yet disappeared from the law in many states. In 1886, the Leavenworth, Kansas, *Standard* reported that "A woman who ran away from her husband at Lawrence some time ago, was found at Fort Leavenworth yesterday by a Lawrence detective and taken back to her home. The officer received a reward of $50 for her capture." [4]

Yet, here too, the tide was turning, and in much of the West and Midwest women enjoyed substantial legal equality, including, in the new state of Wyoming, the right to vote. By 1900,

wives might own and control their separate property in three-fourths of the states; in every state a married woman might dispose by will of her separate property; in about two-thirds of the states she possessed her earnings; in the great majority she might make contracts and bring suit. In many states the law provided that if the wife engaged in business by herself or went outside the home to work, her earnings were her own, but all the fruits of her labor within the household still belonged to the husband. Fathers and mothers had equal guardianship of children in nine states. . . .[5]

One common view of women's proper role in the economy was succinctly expressed by C. W. Marsh, inventor of the Marsh harvester. Writing his autobiography in 1910, at the age of seventy-seven, Marsh echoed the conviction of many in his generation: "Nature made woman weaker, physically and mentally, than man, and also better and more refined. Man, compared with her, is coarse, strong, and aggressive. By confining themselves to the duties for which nature has prepared them, respectively, the better they will harmonize. Let her stay in; let him go out." [6] Throughout the nation, however, the feminist revolt against legal and conventional restrictions on women's freedom was gaining momentum during the nineties. The feminists insisted, among many other things, upon full educational and occupational equality. A few intrepid women were already practicing medicine and law, and engaging in other unwomanly pursuits, but women's place in the economy remained, in most essentials, much the same as it had been in the early years of the nation's history—somewhere between the extreme views of where it ought to be.

Nearly half of all American women still lived on farms in 1890. Like farm women throughout history, they rose before the sun and spent their days as active partners in the family's common work. Just what they did depended on the kind of farm, its income, what other members of the family were able to do, the customs of the locality, and many other circumstances.

Pioneer conditions were rapidly passing in the nineties but were still found in parts of the great plains, the Pacific Coast, and the valleys between. West of the Mississippi, all but the youngest farm women had spent their youth in the great struggle to civilize the wilderness. The work of one farm woman in Western Kansas during the last quarter of the century is described in *Sod and Stubble*, John Ise's biography of his German immigrant mother.[7] In the early years, when her home was a dugout with roof and front wall made of squares of prairie sod, she worked side by side with her husband, planting, harvesting, building, fighting grasshoppers and prairie fires, doing as much of whatever needed to be done as her great vitality permitted. Later, as more settlers moved in, as the farm prospered in good years, and as her sons grew older, the heavy field work was taken over by men—neighbors who helped in exchange for help in their own fields, hired hands, and finally her own sons. But this did not make the woman's work much easier, for the presence of male fieldworkers brought a great increase in the work of processing and cooking food, making clothing, and keeping house.

Other farm tasks remained in her hands. These included the entire care of the kitchen garden and much of the work of caring for cattle, pigs, and poultry—herding cows to pasture and back, hauling well water for animals as well as for kitchen and laundry, feeding pigs, hens, and calves, milking and churning and doctoring. Most of what she needed for housekeeping she had to provide herself. She made brooms, mattresses, and floor mats from straw and corn husks; soap, from lye and tallow; lye, from stove ashes. Lye was indispensable for softening water and hulling corn, as well as for soapmaking. She made almost all the clothing for a family which eventually included eleven children, at first by hand, later with a sewing machine.

The family's food supply depended largely on her efforts. Vegetables, fruits, berries, and melons she grew or gathered in spring and summer and preserved in fall for winter use. The butter she churned and the eggs she gathered served not only as food for the family but as currency to trade for cloth and the few foods and other necessities the farm did not produce. Instead of sugar, they used molasses, which she made by pressing sorghum cane with her husband's help, and boiling the juice. Vinegar, essential for pickling, was the product of molasses, rain water, and yeast. For coffee she made a brew of browned rye grain.

On the rare occasions when members of the family went to town, or took longer trips to visit relatives, food and overnight lodging were always obtained without payment at houses en route. But this too was a charge on the labor of the wife, for she was expected to do as much for all who passed. Likewise, when the burden of sickness required more nursing than one family could provide, all of the women in the area were on call, and the calls were frequent.

John Ise's mother worked for money too. Aside from her contribution to the main cash crops of the farm, she brought in money by doing laundry for bachelors and widowers, by running the community's post office from her kitchen, by selling butter and eggs. As they grew older, her daughters helped in all of these tasks and then turned to schoolteaching to add to the family's cash resources.

On a typical Kansas farm, in short, the work of women provided almost all that was necessary for keeping house, feeding, clothing, and otherwise sustaining the family. This meant that the income from the cash crops could be used to develop the farm, purchase machinery, improve stock, replace dugouts and sod huts with frame houses and out-buildings, put up fences, and still keep up with mortgage payments in years of drought, grasshoppers, or low prices. Without this division of work, few farmers could have survived the years of learning to cope with the unfamiliar soil and climate of the West.

Women's work often provided not only the necessities of the household, but much of the cash for developing the farm as well. Willa Cather pointed out that the first pros-perous, mortgage-free farms in Nebraska were owned by immigrant families whose daughters were not too proud to work as domestics in the nearest town, or even as paid hands on neighboring farms. "The girls I knew," said the narrator of *My Ántonia*, "were always helping to pay for ploughs and reapers, brood-sows, or steers to fatten." [8]

Over much of the rural South, still impoverished a quarter century after the Civil War, conditions were at least as primitive as in the West. On the frontier, women worked in the fields only during the first crucial years of establishing a farm, but on the poorer farms of the South both white and Negro women often performed heavy field work throughout their lives. As in the West, daughters could add to the family's cash income by teaching, but the mores of the South usually proscribed domestic employ-ment for white women. For the daughters of poor white farmers, the cotton mills, then springing up in the Southern countryside, offered the main chance to earn money. Ne-gro women, both single and married, worked for pay as farm hands or domestic servants. There were 2.7 million Negro girls and women over ten years of age in 1890,

the great majority of them in the rural South. At least a
million of them were working, half in agriculture, half in
domestic service.

On the old and prosperous farms of the middle Atlantic
states and of the region bounded by the Ohio, the Mississippi, and the Great Lakes, life was easier for men, women,
and children alike. But in these areas, too, women made a
large contribution to the agricultural economy. The Cuv-
verly farm in Monmouth County, New Jersey, supported
some thirty people during the latter part of the nineteenth
century—three generations of the family and a dozen hired
hands. It was a diversified farm, with pigs the major source
of cash income. The work of the women included "cleaning, . . . washing, cooking, preserving, canning, butter-
making, . . . the care of poultry . . . , dressmaking and
the making of men's shirts and overalls." The products of
women's work were bartered for most of the household
necessities the farm did not produce. Butter, eggs, preserved
fruits, and nuts were traded for "cotton material for clothes,
baking powder, raisins, rice, cheese, crackers, pots, pans,
dishes, and hardware." The customary work of the Cuv-
verly women also included the washing, for use as sausage
casing, of the intestines of the 200 hogs that were slaughtered
each year, the manufacture of sausage, lard, and scrapple,
and preparing the hams and shoulders for salting, pickling,
and smoking.[9]

Most farm women worked hard as part of a family enterprise, but a large group, perhaps a quarter of a million, ran
farms on their own. The great majority were widows;
some were married to men no longer able to work; and
there were even a few thousand resolute single women

among them. One observer reported in 1886 that women had taken up claims on public land in all parts of the West. "All over the thinly settled portions of Dakota," she wrote, "women live alone in their own shack and garden patch." [10]

When a family moved to the city, the man found a world of work unlike any he had known before. But the woman continued to work in and around the home, and to do many of the same things she had done on the farm. There is no way of calculating how much of the goods and services enjoyed by urban families were provided by the labors of women about the home, but there is no doubt that it was a substantial part of the total.

Except in the crowded tenement districts of the large cities—which housed a small fraction of the total urban population—town and city dwellers often produced some of their own food. Especially in the coal and steel regions, the grounds around the urban and suburban house sometimes looked much like a rural farmyard. Many families kept chickens or rabbits, sometimes pigs or goats, and even a cow or two, and raised vegetables and fruits in their own garden plots. A study of 2,500 families living in the principal coal, iron, and steel regions in 1890 suggests that about half of them had livestock, poultry, vegetable gardens, or all three. Nearly 30 percent purchased no vegetables other than potatoes during the course of a year.[11] Describing the anthracite coal region of Pennsylvania in 1904, Peter Roberts wrote that "it is interesting to pass along the Schuylkill and Tremont valleys and see the many little farms which are cultivated by mine employees of the Philadelphia and Reading Coal and Iron Company. In the strike of 1902, hundreds of mine employee's families could not have carried on the fight were it not for the small farms and large gardens they cultivate." [12]

Though only a few miles from the center of the greatest metropolis in the land, Queens County and much of Brooklyn were still semirural in 1890, and many families were as dependent on small-scale agriculture as on the industrial or commercial employment of the men of the family. North of what is now the midtown area, Manhattan itself was more bucolic than urban, and pigs and goats were often seen along the East River as far south as Forty-second Street. [13] At a time when men worked ten or twelve hours a day, six days a week, much of the care of urban livestock and gardens inevitably fell to women—quite apart from the fact that such tasks were theirs by tradition.

Most purchased foods came into the urban home in their natural, unprocessed, uncanned, unpackaged state. Perhaps the majority of wives undertook a strenuous annual bout of preserving, pickling, canning, and jelly-making, and most baking was done in the family kitchen. Among 7,000 working-class families investigated by the U.S. Bureau of Labor between 1889 and 1892, less than half purchased any bread, and almost all bought huge amounts of flour, an average of more than 1,000 pounds per family per year. Even among the families of skilled craftsmen, who earned more than most other workingmen, one fourth bought no bread, and flour consumption averaged over two pounds per family per day. [14]

No respectable home in 1890 was without a well-used sewing machine—one of the first items widely sold on the installment plan. Most men's clothing was bought, but most of the clothing of women and children was still made at

home. In addition, there were curtains and sheets to be
hemmed, caps and sweaters and stockings to be knitted
and darned. Every prospective mother was expected to
knit and sew a complete wardrobe for her first child, and to
replenish it thereafter as needed.

Whether in the country or the city, houses were cleaned
and clothing laundered without benefit of electrical appliances. Foods were cooked and houses warmed by stoves
which were stoked and cleaned by women. In most homes
hot water was available only by heating it on the kitchen
range, frequently only after carrying it from a tap down
the hall or from a well in the yard.

Sickness and death were more familiar in 1890 than they
are today. Diptheria and pneumonia were common in
winter, and in many areas malaria was epidemic in summer.
Without modern drugs, sickness was often prolonged. Unlike most rural areas, cities had doctors and hospitals. But
the doctor was rarely called unless the patient was critically
ill, and the only patients in most hospitals were paupers
without relatives or friends to save them from the most
feared of urban institutions. There were probably less than
500 trained nurses in the entire nation. As in the country,
therefore, most of the burden of medical care fell on the
women of the family.

The ability to carry on these and other household economic activities was an important criterion of a good wife
in 1890, even among the well-to-do. Maude Nathan lived
in a fashionable New York brownstone, with a staff of
four servants, during the 1880's and 1890's. When she began to
work with women's organizations on behalf of social reform,
her husband's family was disturbed. Her autobiography
tells how she sought to allay their misgivings and prove her

womanliness by devoting herself diligently to household duties. She did all the marketing, purchased materials for and planned and supervised the home manufacture of linens, underwear, and her own dresses and hats, closely supervised the servants, and, once a year, put up a year's supply of pickles, preserves, and corned beef.[15]

In addition to producing goods and services for direct use by the family, city women earned money by working at home in a great many ways. Perhaps the most common way was to take in boarders. Many of the new residents of the towns and cities in 1890 were young, unmarried men and women whose families remained in the country or in Europe. Others were immigrant husbands who had left their wives and children behind until they could save enough to send for them. Most of these people found board and lodging with private families. In 1910, 4.5 million persons, 5 percent of the nation's population, lived with families they were not related to. There were, on the average, two such persons for every ten households.[16]

Among the 7,000 working-class families studied by the U.S. Bureau of Labor around 1890, nearly one fifth had boarders.[17] Half of the working-class households covered by a 1907 study in New York City contained one or more boarders.[18] In some isolated mill villages, such as Perry, in western New York, taking in boarders was the major industry of the householders. Almost every house in Perry contained half a dozen or more of the young men and women who had come from farms for miles around to work in the town's woolen mill.[19] Immigrant and low-income families were most likely to take in boarders. Sometimes a family had only one or two boarders in a separate room. Sometimes family and boarders lived together, two in a bed, six or eight in a room, and up to twenty or thirty in one small house or flat.

Sewing was the second most important way that women earned money by working at home. Even small towns usually supported at least one dressmaker and milliner, and, in a day when household thrift was honored, there was also money to be made by mending and "making over." The ready-made clothing industry was still in the midst of the transition from domestic to factory manufacture. To the independent seamstress, it was a rapidly growing competitor, but to thousands of other women in and near all the larger towns and cities it was an abundant source of home work.

The collar-and-cuff capital of the nation, Troy, New York, provided an enormous volume of home work. At the turn of the century, according to one account, there was "not a town within thirty miles . . . wherein a portion of the female population is not engaged in . . . collar and cuff manufacture. . . ." The companies ran regular stage routes to deliver raw materials and pick up finished work. Usually, they financed the purchase of sewing machines, arranging for repayment in weekly installments. In this way, continues the description, "many a wife and mother can earn little comforts for her family. . . ." [20]

In New York, Chicago, and other major cities, home work in the garment industry was more likely to be a way of surviving than a matter of earning little comforts. Lucia Machiarulo was one of thousands of immigrant wives who worked for clothing manufacturers in the tenements of New York's lower East Side. During the depression which began in 1893, her husband worked irregularly as a day laborer, but most of the family's income was earned by sewing buttons and seams on trousers. She and a fifteen-year-old daughter worked 18 hours a day, sharing the sewing, perfunctory housekeeping, and the care of four younger children. When there was plenty of work, when the baby was well, and when the husband helped with the needle because he had no other job, they sometimes earned as much as $5.50 a week.[21]

Many of the Bohemian and German families of New York's upper East Side made cigars at home. Manufacturers bought or leased whole blocks of tenements, rented them to families, supplied each apartment with tobacco, and subtracted the rent from the families' earnings. Usually the whole family worked. Younger children worked after school and on weekends, stripping tobacco from the stems. Older children and parents made and packed cigars.[22]

There were dozens of other ways in which urban housewives earned money in the 1890's. The Census counted over 200,000 laundresses, most of whom were Negro women working in their own homes or the homes of their employers, and thousands of women who were not counted also took in laundry more or less regularly. Wives often provided laundry service as well as food for boarders. In 1902, two thirds of the employment agencies in New York, Boston, Philadelphia, and Chicago were run by women, usually in their homes, and another 10 percent were run by husband and wife jointly.[23] Most of these agencies specialized in supplying domestic help. During the eighties and nineties women's exchanges were founded in many of the larger cities to sell such homemade products as

hand-painted and embroidered tapestries . . . , artistic screens . . . , elaborately decorated china . . . , textile fabrics . . . made up into articles for wall decorations, bed and table use, or per-

sonal wear . . . , cakes, pickles, preserves, and other edibles. . . .
In . . . one establishment [in New York City] the sales for
the year 1888 amounted to $51,180.26. . . . Most of those con-
tributing articles to the exchanges for sale were "reduced gen-
tlewomen," who made use of this means of becoming their own
employers, not so much for support, as to better their conditions . . . without the publicity consequent upon working for
manufacturers.[24]

Domestic service was the oldest and still the largest of
the occupations pursued by women outside the circle of
their own families. The 1890 Census counted about 1.2
million women working as housekeepers, chambermaids,
cooks, charwomen, servants, etc. Some worked in institutions and office buildings, but the great majority worked
in private homes, and most of them "lived in." Half of the
women in domestic service were of foreign parentage, and
another fourth were Negroes. Only 100,000 were married,
and most of these were Negro women. Widows outnumbered wives, but the great majority were young, single
girls, working as servants only until they married.

The largest field of women's work unequivocally separate from the home was unskilled and semiskilled factory
employment. Every generation of Americans seems to think
that the most recent war was responsible for introducing
women into the factory. Actually, women were an important part of the factory work force long before World
War II, or World War I, or even the Civil War. Indeed,
when factories first appeared on the American scene in
early nineteenth-century New England, the work was
quickly identified as peculiarly suited for women, or, rather,
for girls. Spinning and weaving had been women's work
long before the advent of the new textile mills. Work in
the mills was not particularly strenuous or hard to learn.

The long hours of work and the strictly cloistered life the mill girls were required to lead after hours seemed to provide sufficient protection from the unique temptations of town life. For these and other reasons, mill work was generally regarded as a desirable way to preserve young women from the moral perils of idleness, and at the same time add to the wealth of the community without drawing men and boys away from more important work in agriculture.[25]

From that day on, women have been an essential element in the manufacturing labor force. In 1890, at least one million women worked in factories. They outnumbered men in the clothing factories. They made up about half the labor force in the textile mills and tobacco factories, and were a substantial minority in the shoe, food processing, and many other industries. Most women factory hands worked in light industries related to women's traditional household duties: spinning, weaving, sewing, cooking. But many were also employed in foundries, tin plate mills, print shops, metal fabricating plants, and other kinds of factories which are still popularly viewed as masculine territory. This does not mean that men and women were hired and assigned without regard to sex. On the contrary, particular jobs were almost invariably known as men's or women's jobs, even though the reasons for assigning some jobs to women may be difficult to appreciate today.

Thus, "opening" tin plate sheets was women's or boys', but never men's, work in the Pittsburgh area. The opener had to catch fifty-pound stacks of six to eight sheets, firmly stuck together as they emerged hot from the rollers, bang them on the floor to loosen the sheets, and then forcibly tear the sheets apart with gloved hands while kneeling on the stack to hold it down. The work day was ten hours.[26] Few women held such strenuous jobs, however. Most of them made or assembled small, light objects, tended semi-automatic machines, packed, labled, inspected, or performed similar tasks. Generally, their jobs required little skill and provided low pay and few chances for advancement.

The typical female factory worker was much like the typical white domestic servant—young, single, an immigrant or the daughter of immigrants. Few factories employed Negro women, and, except in the New England textile towns, few married women worked in factories. The Bureau of Labor's 1887 study of 17,000 women factory workers in large cities found that three fourths of them were under twenty-five, and only 4 percent were married. Three out of four were foreign born or of foreign parentage.[27]

A quarter of a million schoolteachers made up the only other large group of women employed outside of their homes. The replacement of men by women in the nation's classrooms had begun as early as the 1830's. Until late in the century there were virtually no other jobs for women with some education and middle-class status or aspirations. Consequently, there was an abundant supply of young women willing to teach for one half to one third of what men teachers received. In 1890 women teachers outnumbered men by about two to one. Like domestics and factory workers, most teachers were young and single. Only one woman teacher out of twenty-five was married, partly because many communities would not employ married women. "Should a female teacher marry," declared the by-laws of New York City, "her place shall thereupon become vacant." [28] Well over half of all women teachers were under twenty-five. Unlike domestic and factory workers, however, the great majority of teachers were of native stock.

Teaching was the only profession employing many women. Indeed, in most parts of the country there was little reason to call teaching a profession. Most schoolteachers had only six or eight years of elementary education, and it was not until 1907 that Indiana became the first state to require that all licensed teachers be high school graduates. In three of the North Central states, only about 10 percent of the teachers (men and women) during the 1891–92 school year were normal school or college graduates.[29] As Nicholas Murray Butler described them, the normal schools were no more than two-year "high schools with a slight infusion of pedagogic instruction." [30]

Nursing, of course, had always been a woman's occupation, but there were not many paid nurses in 1890. Most of the 40,000 nurses and midwives counted by the Census had no formal training, and even the few hundred who had graduated from hospital nursing schools had only a smattering of instruction. Their training usually consisted of one year of ward nursing under the supervision of a second-year student serving as head nurse, and then a second year as head nurse before they went out into private practice. The status of the profession near the end of the decade is indicated by the fact that responsibility for nursing during the Spanish-American War was assigned to the Daughters of the American Revolution, even though the members of the Nurses' Associated Alumni, forerunner of the American Nurses Association, had volunteered their services.[31]

With the dubious exceptions of teaching and nursing the professions remained almost entirely a man's world. A few

hundred women had succeeded in obtaining medical training, largely because of the development of gynecology and
obstetrics. The nineteenth-century mind balked at permitting women to study anatomy, especially in the presence
of men, but it had almost as much difficulty with the idea
of permitting men doctors to replace midwives. One way
out of this dilemma was to establish separate medical
schools for women. Most of these provided a poor excuse
for medical training, but by 1890 three schools were providing adequate preparation, by the standards of the time,
to a total enrollment of 360 women. Three medical schools
for men had also opened their doors to women. The medical
school at the University of Michigan solved the problem of
mixed classes by arranging duplicate lectures in all subjects
likely to create embarrassment.[32]

The situation was much the same in law. Between 1870
and 1890 all states admitted women to the bar. One side in
the accompanying controversy declared that women must
not be sullied by the harsh and degrading aspects of legal
practice. The other side stressed not only women's rights
to equal educational opportunity, but the need for women
lawyers to serve the needs of women clients.[33] By 1890, the
census counted some 200 women lawyers.

The whole realm of commerce and the white-collar side
of industry were still male preserves, but not as exclusively
as they had once been. After the Civil War, women made
a small breech in these masculine strongholds, and by 1890
they were beginning to pour into stores and offices. Girls
who dressed neatly and could speak reasonably good English were welcomed in the department stores of the larger
cities. Most of them began as cash girls, who carried the

customer's money to the cashier and returned with change. They also worked as stock clerks, package wrappers, mail-order clerks, and saleswomen.

As in manufacturing, men and women were rarely hired for the same kinds of work. E. W. Bloomingdale declared in 1895 that there was not a woman in Bloomingdale Brothers who did the same work as men.[34] Women sales clerks were usually found in the bargain basement, in other departments which carried low-priced items and did not require wide knowledge of the stock, and in departments which sold women's clothing and accessories. By the end of the century, a few women had become buyers, usually in women's wear departments, but almost all other super-visors were men. There were 100,000 women retail sales clerks by 1890, not many compared to the half million males, but three times as many as in 1880, and ten times more than in 1870.

The 1890 office usually showed its masculine background —dark, dingy, often dirty, and amply supplied with spit-toons. The spittoon, however, was doomed by the presence of some 75,000 women office workers, about equally divided among bookkeepers, clerks, and the advance guard of the coming horde of typists and stenographers. Still outnumbered by men in all other office jobs, women had already fixed their hold on the recently perfected type-writer. Twice as many women as men were working as typists and stenographers, and most of the men were stenographers rather than typists. Like most women working outside their homes in 1890, those who worked in offices and stores were very young, and almost all were single. Most of the office workers were of native parentage. Selling, however, was the first step up from domestic and factory work for the daughters of immigrants, and over half the women sales clerks had immigrant parents.

How many women were engaged in each of the different kinds of work described in the preceding pages is known only roughly. Most of the nation's 11 million wives worked long and diligently to raise their families' plane of living. In addition to their unpaid work, most of the 4 to 5 million farm wives brought in some money by working at home, and so did a great many other married women. Very few wives were employed away from home. Among the 4 million working girls and women counted by the 1890 Census, only half a million were married. It is difficult, however, to say just what this figure means. It includes women working for money both within and outside their homes, and there is reason to believe that the Census failed to count a great many women in both groups. One can only guess that about 5 percent of all married women held jobs that took them away from their homes and families.

Only among Negroes and among the immigrant populations of New England textile towns were a large minority of wives employed outside of the home. By and large, the married women who did work away from home were those whose husbands were permanently or temporarily unable to support their families. There were, as a matter of fact, more widows than wives working regularly for pay in 1890. Of the nearly 20 million women over fifteen in the country, more than 2 million were widows, and the Census counted 630,000 of them as gainfully occupied.

Many single girls spent their time helping their mothers. Nevertheless, about half of all women worked for pay outside the home during part of the eight to ten years after they left school and before they married. Of the 6 million

single girls and women over fifteen, 2.5 million were gainfully employed, according to the Census. At least another
quarter of a million girls under fifteen were also working
for pay. Single women constituted the great majority—
perhaps three fourths—of all women who worked for pay
outside the home.

Their occupations are easily identified: domestic service,
farm labor, unskilled or semiskilled factory work (mainly
in textile and garment manufacturing), and schoolteaching
accounted for the overwhelming majority. In teaching,
domestic service, and the branches of manufacturing which
employed the largest numbers of women, they outnumbered male workers. A still small, but rapidly growing,
number of women were working as sales clerks and in office
jobs. A few women were serving women clients in medicine
and law. A few widows had succeeded to the management
of their husbands' businesses. By and large, however, commerce, management, the professions, the skilled trades—all
of the responsible, well-paid jobs in the modern urban
economy—were in the hands of men.

By 1890 a great many men no longer worked at home.
More than two fifths of all men still worked on farms, but
the great majority of the others set out for work early in
the morning, six days out of every seven, and did not return
for ten or twelve hours. Today, almost all men work away
from home, and so do a great many women. As we have
seen, more than a third of all women are now in the labor
force, and the great majority of them work outside the
home.

One principal reason for the separation of both men's

and women's work from the home has been the sharp decline in the proportion of the population engaged in farming. The farm is the last stronghold of the family as an
economic unit, but of the 43 million families in the nation
in 1956, only about 4 million earned income by operating
farms, and less than one million depended entirely upon
such income. The other 3 million farming families had additional income from other sources, mainly wages or salaries.

Migration from farm to city, of course, had profound
effects on women's work. In the city, the woman was no
longer a partner in the family's common work, and she
was less and less likely to earn money and contribute to her
family's food supply through gardening, raising poultry,
and similar activities. There were also important changes,
stemming largely from the development of the truck, automobile, and highway, in the work of women who remained
on farms. With the city or its growing suburbs within easy
reach, she no longer had to rely so heavily on her own
efforts to provide what the family needed. Moreover,
changes in agricultural technology decreased the opportunity and the need for her regular or occasional participation in farm work.

In towns and cities, other changes removed much of
women's traditional work from the home. Their opportunities to earn money through home work were severely restricted. The demand for room and board in private homes
fell sharply. There were 25 million more households in the
United States in 1950 than in 1910, but a million and a
quarter fewer nonrelatives living in them.[35] One reason
for this was that there were not so many young, single men
and women working and living apart from their families.

This, in turn, reflected a number of developments, including the restriction of immigration and the fact that young people were staying in school longer and marrying earlier.

Even in 1890, opportunities for women to earn money at home were being narrowed by laws regulating or forbidding home work, especially in the garment, tobacco, and food industries. More important, however, was the growing competition of the factory, which could make clothing, cigars, cigarettes, pickles, and preserves, bake bread, cake, and cookies, wash and iron clothing, and perform many other tasks much more efficiently than women working at home.

The growth of commercial enterprise in fields of work which had always engaged housewives has done much more than deprive some women of opportunities to earn money at home. As prepared foods, ready-made clothing, and commercial laundry services became widely available at reasonable cost, more and more women took advantage of them to reduce the time and labor devoted to providing goods and services for their own families. Because of the perfection of a variety of household appliances and conveniences, the traditional services that women continue to perform in the home are accomplished more quickly and much more easily. In 1890, the sewing machine and the egg beater were about the only mechanical aids in most homes. One is apt to think, in this connection, of such appliances as washing machines and vacuum cleaners, but central heating and hot and cold running water have probably done as much to ease women's work as all of the mechanical cleaning devices combined.

All of these developments might be summarized by saying that the work of women within the home, like the rest of the nation's work, has been transformed by the advance of industry. Small-scale domestic production has given way to mass production for a wide market; human energy, to mechanical and electrical. And for women as for men, the new ways of working have saved much time and more effort.

The transformation of women's work, however, has been the result of much more than the advance of industry and trade. Developments in science and technology, in attitudes and aspirations, in social structure and family living patterns have all contributed. Consider, for instance, the burdens of motherhood. Today's young mother can have little notion of the time and physical and emotional resources consumed by motherhood in 1890. The average mother today bears two or three children, compared to five or six borne by mothers living before the turn of the century. Because better health and medical care have reduced miscarriages and stillbirths, the number of pregnancies has decreased still more. For the same reasons, and also because most mothers are now able to avoid hard physical work before and after childbirth, each pregnancy is much less likely to lead to sickness, disability, or death. Because of uncontaminated water supplies, pure food and drug laws, modern sanitation, insect controls, new immunizing agents and drugs, central heating, better nutrition—to say nothing of hospital facilities and skilled medical care—today's mother is likely to escape the strain of nursing each of her children through a series of severe illnesses, and the still greater strain of burying one or more of them. Feeding and clothing children, of course, have become much easier. Finally, the extension of the school day, the school year, and the number of years spent in school has relieved mothers of much of the necessity for supervising older children.

The time and energy women have saved because they no longer perform a multitude of household tasks, or because they accomplish them more easily, have been put to use in a variety of ways. Many women found new work within the home. A glance at any woman's magazine testifies to the enormous importance of making today's home a place of beauty, culture, and spotless cleanliness; on keeping husbands contented and happy; and on insuring the sound emotional development of children. Clothing and linens that in 1890 might have been used for a week before laundering may now be used no more than a day. Interior decorating, gardening, preparation of varied and attractive menus, personal beauty care, and chauffering, entertaining, supervising, and otherwise catering to children—all take far more time than they used to. The focus of women's tasks at home has shifted. Less occupied with meeting the physical needs of her husband and children, the wife is now expected to help them pursue the elusive goal of happiness. Whether these new duties of women are properly classified as work is a matter of definition. There is no doubt that they consume time and energy, and that society imposes at least some of them upon the woman who esteems her status as wife and mother.

Not all of the newer duties of the housewife are of her own or even society's choosing. The child, once left unattended in fields and woods, can be left in city streets only to his own peril. And the dust, smoke, and soot of the city are perhaps as responsible as rising standards of cleanliness for more frequent housecleaning and laundering.

Another kind of activity to which some woman have turned is volunteer work for health, welfare, and other community agencies. Women's voluntary organizations had a long history even before 1890. The beginnings of hospital reform and of modern nursing in the 1870's were largely the work of committees of public-spirited women, many of whom had helped to provide nursing services during the Civil War. The forerunners of social work were the "friendly visitors" whose duties were to seek out applicants for charity, determine whether they were among the deserving or the undeserving poor, and encourage them, by example, to become upright, self-supporting citizens. In 1892 there were 4,000 volunteers, mostly women, working for charity organization societies.[36]

Before the turn of the century, nevertheless, volunteer work was confined largely to a small group of well-to-do women, who often made it a full-time career. It was not until much later that a different kind of volunteer work evolved, making use of thousands of middle- and working-class women (and men), usually on a part-time basis, in such activities as committee work for parent-teacher associations; fund raising; supervising Boy Scout, Girl Scout, and other organized children's activities; political organizing at the local level; participating in school and community improvement groups; helping to run cooperative nursery schools, and all of the other things that today take so much of the time of many married women.

Some of women's increasing freedom from traditional household tasks has been devoted to purely recreational activities. One critic, a woman whose avowed bias was "that work is a good thing and that women have too much leisure," concluded in 1924, "that machinery products,

canned goods and city crowding cut away from the life of
the average woman . . . many hours of activity, leaving
time that would hang heavily upon her hands, if not filled
by the 'movie,' the casual shopping the object of which is
not to buy but to see, the tea-party, and the gossip fest." [37]
Much earlier, even before 1890, there were signs that some
women were finding time heavy on their hands. European
visitors were shocked by the fact that even in working-class
districts some young wives lived in boarding houses and
spent their days in idle talk, shopping, or reading romantic
novels. Maude Nathan, who became President of the New
York Consumer's League in 1896, took up a career as a
volunteer leader partly out of boredom with a daily routine
which began with a few hours of housekeeping, and was
filled out with singing lessons and embroidery in the morning, and shopping and social calls in the afternoon.[38] The
decline of household work, of course, affected daughters
as well as mothers. The instructions to Census enumerators
in 1890 included the admonition that "the large body of
persons, particularly young women, who live at home and
do nothing," should be distinguished from "daughters who
assist in the household duties." The results of this enumeration, however, were not preserved.[39]

Women's clubs began to multiply rapidly in the 1880's
and were soon providing endless material for humorists and
sober critics who found it amusing, or alarming, that women
should seek entertainment, edification, and social intercourse outside of their own parlors. The General Federation
of Women's Clubs was founded in 1889 and by 1896 em-
braced 495 individual clubs and twenty state federations.[40]
In the following decades American society was permeated
by women's clubs devoted to activities ranging from gossip

and cards through literary study to community service. Today the clubs affiliated with the General Federation claim 5 million members. One aspect of the activities of women's clubs in the 1930's and 1940's was recorded by Helen E. Hokinson in her cartoons depicting the earnest failure of the middle-aged club woman to fathom the intricacies of parliamentary procedure, literature, modern art, alcoholic refreshments, and other appurtenances of sophistication and culture. What the humorists failed to reflect were the successes of women's clubs, both as a way of introducing the kitchen-bound housewife to the problems of the world about her, and as an impetus to voluntary service activities which have become an essential part of the social fabric.

Girls and young women have also found new activities to replace much of their former work as mothers' helpers. In 1890, most boys and girls left school at fourteen, if not before. Today, however, three fourths of the sixteen- and seventeen-year-olds are still attending school. Between 1890 and 1950, moreover, the average number of days spent in school by public school students nearly doubled, from 85 to 160 per year.[41] Like their mothers, girls are also spending more time in organized leisure activities.

In addition to performing new duties at home, entering volunteer work, engaging in a variety of leisure-time activities, and spending more time in school, girls and women were also turning to paid work outside the home. As school attendance was prolonged, and child labor prohibited, fewer young girls held jobs. At the same time, however, more girls were going to work after they left school. By 1940 the girl who did not was exceptional. The net result has been very little change in the proportion of all single girls and women working outside the home. Among married women, however, this proportion has grown steadily. It was probably little more than 5 percent in 1890. By 1940, it was approaching 15 percent. By 1950 it was almost one fourth, and today it is nearing one third.

All of these changes in the activities of women have been most pronounced among the urban and suburban middle classes, which could best afford to buy goods, services, and conveniences to lighten women's traditional work at home. These, moreover, were the families which were most likely to have only one or two children. And they were the first to send their daughters to high school and college, where they often acquired both the qualifications and the desire to engage in activities other than routine housekeeping. Nevertheless, the revolution in women's work has not been confined to this one segment of society. America has long been known as a nation where most families consider themselves middle class, and pattern their behavior accordingly, as far as their resources permit.

The kinds of jobs obtained by women have been determined, in part, by the directions in which the economy was growing, and, therefore, by the kinds of work which became available. The production of physical goods has increased enormously since 1890, but the labor force directly engaged in physical production has not grown proportionately. Both within and outside of manufacturing industries, employment in clerical, secretarial, technical, professional, and managerial occupations has expanded much more than factory employment. In commerce, in government, in such professional service fields as education and health, and in certain personal service industries such as restaurants and entertainment, employment has grown more rapidly than in manufacturing. In general, the rapidly growing areas of work have been those in which technological advances have had less impact on productivity; where more work has required more workers; and where labor costs have accounted for a high proportion of total costs. Some of the occupations covered by this very broad grouping have not attracted many women. There are still, for instances, relatively few women in engineering, medicine, or industrial management. Nevertheless, the most rapid growth of women's employment has occurred within these areas.

Even though women are somewhat more widely distributed throughout manufacturing industry than they were in 1890, women's place in the factory has changed remarkably little. The factory does not now claim a much larger proportion of women workers than it did then. By and large, it remains true that women factory workers are concentrated in the garment, textile, tobacco, and other light, nondurable goods industries, and that they are an important minority in most others. Today, as in 1890, their work is likely to consist of making or assembling small items, packaging, labeling, inspecting, machine-tending. Few have highly skilled or supervisory jobs, for most jobs are still assigned on the basis of sex, and the best ones are still reserved for men.

Less work within the home and increased opportunities for jobs on the outside have affected domestic servants as well as housewives. The population more than doubled between 1890 and 1950, but the number of women holding service jobs in private households remained about one million. The decline in the relative importance of domestic service was paralleled by a substantial rise in employment in related jobs outside the home. Thus, in 1950 more than a million women were employed outside of private homes to cook and serve food and to operate laundry services. Since 1950 employment in private households has increased phenomenally, and now amounts to well over 2 million. It does not seem likely, however, that the number of paid housekeepers and servants has increased nearly this much. Most of the growth in the total number of private household workers can probably be explained as an increase in the number of baby sitters. This, in turn, reflects the growing number of small children in the population, the growing number of teen-agers available for such work, increasing expenditures for recreation, and more careful Census techniques for enumerating casual workers.

In spite of the recent jump in household employment and the steady rise in service employment outside of private homes, manual labor in the service occupations, on the farm, and in the factory now accounts for less than half of all working women, compared to perhaps 85 per cent in 1890. The largest part of the growth in women's employment outside the home has been absorbed by clerical, secretarial, and other office work. In industry, in commerce, in government, and in every other sector of the economy, the expanding scope and complexity of operations has brought a vast increase in the need for record-keeping and communicating—a need which has been met mainly by women, a need, one might add, which has been stimulated by the fact that the women were available. Today some 6 million women work as file clerks, office machine operators, typists, stenographers, secretaries, and in similar office occupations, and such jobs occupy three out of every ten women who work for pay. Another concomitant of the development of a complex industrial society, of course, is an increase in the volume of sales transactions. Although employment in selling has not kept pace with clerical employment, it accounts for another million and a half women.

Factory, farm, service, clerical, and sales occupations employ about seventeen out of every twenty women in today's labor force. Most of the remainder are teachers or nurses. Whatever the deficiencies in the educational and health services now available to Americans, both have grown tremendously during the last seven decades, and both have relied heavily on women workers. There are now over a million women teachers, and another half million registered and student nurses. About three fourths of all teachers and nearly all nurses are women.

In broad outline, then, the picture of women's occupations outside the home has changed since 1890 in only a few essentials: a sharp decline in the relative importance of manual work on farm, in factory, and in household service occupations; and sharp increases in the importance of clerical and sales work, teaching and nursing, and nonhousehold service jobs. There are still relatively few women in managerial positions and in the traditionally male professions. Nevertheless, there have been very substantial gains, especially during the last two decades, in the number of women working as doctors, lawyers, engineers, scientists, executives, and managers. Several professional and semiprofessional fields which have always been the acknowledged territory of women—including social work, library service, and a number of medical-technical specialties—have also grown quite remarkably.

Other important developments become apparent only if one looks behind the titles of occupations that have changed in almost every way but name. Today's teacher, with her B.A. and perhaps her M.A. degree, bears little resemblance to the elementary school graduates who staffed most schoolrooms in 1890. Her competence, pay, status, and working conditions are all vastly improved, and the same is true of nurses. One might even say that in each of these ways, today's clerical worker stands far in advance of 1890's teacher or nurse.

Far more striking than any changes in the kinds of work done by women in the labor force is the shift of wives and mothers from household activities to the world of paid employment. Emphasis on the new work of women, however, should not be allowed to obscure an equally important fact. Today, as always, most of the time and effort of American wives is devoted to their responsibilities within the home and the family circle. This is true even of those who are in the labor force. Since 1890 the demands of paid work have become much lighter. The normal work week has decreased from sixty to forty hours; paid holidays and vacations have become universal; and most of the hard, physical labor that work once required has been eliminated. Because of these developments, many women can work outside the home and still have time and energy left for home and family. Moreover, most working mothers do not assume the burdens of a full schedule of paid work. Among employed mothers of preschool children, four out of five worked only part time or less than half the year in 1956. Among those whose children were in school, three out of five followed the same curtailed work schedule. And even among working wives who had no children at home, only a little more than half were year-round, full-time members of the labor force.

Chapter II
THE WOMEN
WHO WORK

THE TYPICAL 1890 working woman is easily sketched. She was young and single, the daughter of ambitious, hard-working immigrants or native farmers. With little education or training, she was spending the years between school and marriage in one of the many kinds of unskilled jobs available in the city. The main variations from this type can also be readily discerned: widows, wives whose husbands did not support them, Negro women in farm or domestic service jobs in the South, immigrant wives in the cotton mills of the North, and a few unconventional women who worked even though others in similar circumstances did not.

During the last quarter of the nineteenth century, girls born into native white families of some social standing rarely worked outside their homes. By keeping his daughter at school or at home a father protected her from the defeminizing influence of the harsh world of work, saved her the embarrassment of associating with men to whom she had not been properly introduced, safeguarded her delicate constitution, and proved to the world that he was capable of providing for all his family's wants. When

Maude Nathan's class graduated from high school in Green Bay, Wisconsin, some of her friends went to work as teachers or salesgirls. Yet, she wrote, "although my father was by no means in affluent circumstances, and although my mother found it necessary to economize in many ways, there was no thought . . . of my adding to the family income by taking a position. I was permitted to assume certain domestic duties and to . . . keep the pantry key. . . . I was taught to cook and sew and was sent twice a week to a convent to learn to embroider." [1] The difference between Maude Nathan and her classmates was that her family was still living by the standards appropriate to the wealth and social position they had recently lost.

In a society as ambitious and mobile as the United States, what the upper classes did became the aspiration of those below them. But keeping young girls close to the family hearth was only one mark of social standing. Another was having money to spend after necessities were paid for. And one of the principal ways of augmenting the father's earnings was to send daughters as well as sons to work.

Shortly after the turn of the century, for instance, one student of family life recorded the changing budget of a family whose income had recently increased from $800 to $1,365 a year. They were described as "ambitious, fairly educated people. . . . The horizon of comfortable living is broadening. Their wants keep pace and overstep the growing income. . . . The family had moved from a flat for which they paid $10 a month, to a flat of five good-sized rooms with well-equipped bathroom at $20." Their expenditures for food advanced from $7 to $11 a week. "To see the mother and daughter on the street, one might easily judge their clothes the expression of a $3,500 household.

. . . They had a piano and a sideboard . . . and the furnishings and bric-a-brac gave the atmosphere of a well-
to-do family in a small town." The changes in their standard
of living were made possible by the fact that the father, a
shipping clerk, had received a $200 increase, and a daughter
had taken a job for $365 a year as a salesgirl in a clothing
shop.[2]

Many girls went to work for more personal reasons than
the desire to add to the family's comforts and social standing. The years around the turn of the century were a
period of rapid change and exciting possibilities for young
women. The urban economy offered them an increasing
variety of opportunities to earn money. At the same time,
new and more liberal views of women's abilities, characteristics, and place in life gave them a chance to move about
more freely in the community, act more independently, and
broaden their experience. For the most part, however, these
possibilities were confined to the few years of late adolescence and early adulthood, before the young woman married and began to raise a family. By the hundreds of
thousands young women were spending these years in jobs
which gave them new experiences, new friends, and some
money of their own. Dreiser's Sister Carrie was one of them.
In 1889 she came from rural Illinois to Chicago because she
was bored at home and because Chicago seemed a romantic
place. She found work in a shoe factory because she had
to work if she was to stay there.

Mrs. John Van Vorst, a young Boston society matron
with a strong social conscience, set out in 1902 to investigate the conditions of working girls by posing as one of
them. Prepared to find "one vast class of slaves, miserable
drudges, doomed to dirt, ugliness, and overwork," she got

a job as a sewing-machine operator in the largest plant in a small factory town near Buffalo.

> Now what [she asked herself] is the mill's attraction and what is the power of this small town? Its population is 3,346. Of these, 1,000 work in the knitting mill, 200 more in a cutlery factory, and 300 in various flour, butter, barrel, planing mills, and salt blocks. Half the inhabitants are young hands. Not one in a hundred has a home in Perry; they have come from all Western parts of the state to work. . . . It is a town of youthful contemporaries, stung with America's ambition for independence and adventure. . . .

And yet, she added, the girls were defensive about their employment, repeatedly explaining,

> I don't have to work, my father gives me all the money I need, but not all . . . I want. I like to be independent and spend my money as I please.[3]

To many girls, spending money as they pleased meant spending most of it on clothing. It is now taken for granted that working women dress very much like other women. This was also more or less true in 1890, but it was not yet taken for granted. When Marie Van Vorst joined her sister-in-law in masquerading as a working girl, she donned what she thought was an appropriate costume of plain appearance and cheap but serviceable material. To her chagrin, however, she found that her dress made her an object of sympathy among the girls and women in the shoe factories of Lynn, Massachusetts.[4] To the Van Vorsts and to most other middle- and upper-class observers, the working girl's extravagant expenditures on clothing were one of the major social and moral problems of the day, especially since extravagance was often carried over into married life. "This craving for many and varied dresses is fatal to social

progress," wrote one student of working-class life. "It de-
vours the wages of the man, condemns many women to a
single life, and leads to sterility after marriage. The gown
and the hat bring domestic infelicity into the homes of men
who are anxious to pay their bills and lead an honest life." [5]

Moral judgments aside, the conclusion that many girls
worked to pay for their wardrobes was not unfounded. The
Bureau of Labor's 1887 study of urban working girls found
that they spent, on the average, $80 a year, more than a
quarter of their earnings, on clothing. In a day when $10
would buy all that Marie Van Vorst wore to the shoe factory, including winter coat, $80 represented a wardrobe
of considerable variety and elegance, especially if it were
invested, not in ready-made clothing, but in materials to
make and remake one's own clothing.

If the young woman of 1890 wanted to be a lady, she had
to stay home; but going to work could at least allow her to
dress like a lady, and could make life pleasanter in a great
many other ways as well. The choice between staying home
and going to work was influenced by many circumstances.
Most important was her family's financial situation. If she
was left as the sole support of younger brothers and sisters
or of aged parents, she had no alternative. The broken-
hearted spinster who bravely sacrificed her youth and her
chance for marriage in order to support and care for brothers, sisters, or parents was for long a favorite theme of
American fiction. Rose Haggerty was one of these "prisoners of poverty" whose stories were told in a series of articles
in the Sunday New York *Tribune* during the 1880's. When
she was fourteen, Rose's father, mother, and brother died
in an epidemic. As the oldest of five girls, Rose went to
work in a bag factory for $3 a week, leaving the children

to look after each other. After years of struggle, she refused an eligible suitor rather than abandon her sisters. Eventually, defeated and penniless, she turned to prostitution as an easier and surer way of feeding her family.[6] Whether the ending was typical or not, the rest of the story was not an uncommon one.

When a family was not supported by the father, the obligation to work fell on older sons, older daughters, younger sons, and younger daughters, in that order. The mother was usually the last to take a job. Fannie Harris, aged thirteen, was one of the children who worked because her father could not. She had been employed for six months in a necktie factory, earning $2 for a 60 hour week, when she was called to testify before a special committee of the New York legislature in 1895. Part of her testimony follows:

Q. What did you do with that two dollars? *A.* Gave it to my mamma.

Q. Did your mamma give you anything to spend? *A.* Yes, sir . . . two cents every week. . . .

Q. Now, have you been to school in this country? *A.* No. . . .

Q. Can you spell cat? . . . *A.* I forgot.

Q. When did you have a birthday? . . . *A.* I never had a birthday because we haven't any money to make a birthday. . . .

Q. Is your papa an old man? *A.* Yes, sir.

Q. Have you got any older brothers and sisters? *A.* I have an older sister.

Q. Does she work? *A.* Yes, sir.

Q. Does your mamma work? *A.* Now she ain't working because I am working, but before, when I didn't work, she worked. . . .

Q. Does your papa do anything; does he work? *A.* Yes, sir; he works, but just now he is not at work—he is sick.

Q. Who told you that you must not work? *A.* A lady told me; an inspector came up and told me I must not work because I was too young. . . . She said I should go to school. . . .

Q. Did you tell your mamma about it? *A.* Mamma said I couldn't go to school.[7]

Fannie Harris was not among the most pathetic of the working children of the time. Snuff-chewing, hard-swearing, undernourished little girls of seven and eight worked from six in the morning to seven at night in some of the cotton mills of the South. Marie Van Vorst described the scene during the half hour lunch break in a South Carolina mill:

The children crouch on the floor by the frames; some fall asleep between the mouthfuls of food, and so lie asleep with food in their mouths until the overseer raises them to their tasks again. . . . I asked the little girl who teaches me to spool who the man is whom I have seen riding around on horseback through the town. "Why, he goes roun' rousin' up the hands who ain't in their places. Sometimes he takes the children outen thayre bades an' brings 'em back to the mill." [8]

Dire poverty was not the only, nor even the major, explanation for the employment of little girls. One of the seven-year-olds in the South Carolina mill was the daughter of the town's most prosperous citizen, a widower, a salesman of sewing machines and parlor organs, and the proprietor of the town's only boarding house. His mother-in-law ran the boarding house, and he also received the mill wages of a thirteen-year-old niece who lived with the family. This was not just an isolated instance of avarice. The records of the state bureaus of labor are full of examples of young working children from families which could

well have afforded to let them go to school.[9] Outside of
Southern mill villages, children as young as seven and eight
were rarely employed, especially if they were girls. Yet in
many places in the North as well as the South, it was customary for most children to go to work at twelve or
fourteen, or as soon as they finished six or eight years of
school.

Whatever their age, most employed girls were the daughters of manual workers whose earnings were modest. Nevertheless, most older working girls were not from poverty-
stricken homes. Among the 17,000 who were interviewed
by the U.S. Bureau of Labor in 1887, nine out of ten lived
with their families, three out of four in homes rated as
"comfortable" by the investigators. On the average, there
were five persons in each family, three of whom were
working.

To the mass of Cleveland's working girls [the report declared,
with some exaggeration] labor is less a necessity than a means
of outside income. The large iron, coal, and oil interests of the
city give employment to thousands of men who are able to
maintain their families, yet whose daughters are self-supporting.
. . . Separate houses, good sanitation, comfortable surroundings,
and general respectability are the rule . . . and extreme poverty
is rarely witnessed.[10]

Whether a single girl worked or not depended almost as
much on where she lived as on how much her father earned.
In most rural areas there were few jobs for women other
than servant or teacher, and few girls worked. In most cities,
on the other hand, the proportion of single girls and women
at work was about as high as it is today. In some of the
textile centers of New England it was even higher. In
Lowell and Fall River, for instance, two out of every three

unmarried girls and women aged ten years and over were employed. In cities like Pittsburgh or Scranton, which depended on heavy industry or mining, there were fewer jobs for women, and only about one third of the single girls worked. In small, heavy-industry towns which lacked the big stores, food-processing plants, and garment factories found in every big city, a girl had no more chance to work than if she had lived on a farm. Almost all of the jobs in Homestead, Pennsylvania, for instance, were within the walls of the Carnegie iron and steel works, and hardly any women were employed.[11]

Although farm girls had little opportunity to work as long as they remained at home, they were, on the whole, more eager to work than girls born and brought up in cities. Like the woolen mill in Perry, New York, which has already been mentioned, a factory had only to open its doors in any part of the rural United States to find itself besieged by girls and young women from miles around, all eager for work. Rather than wait for the factory to come to them, moreover, girls were moving from farm to city jobs in a steady stream. The reasons are not hard to find. The average farm girl was accustomed to long hours of hard manual labor. It did not occur to her that a factory job might be beneath her dignity. She and her family saw in the factory a chance to increase their cash earnings, and to insure a more stable income, independent of the weather and the extreme fluctuations of the agricultural market.

This was an opportunity which appealed even to prosperous farm families. The more primitive and poverty-stricken its background, the more avidly the rural family seized on the chance to earn its share of the wealth dispensed by the factory. In the South, "a family whose crops often did not pay the store accounts, whose members handled almost no money, heard with amazement of . . . twenty-five dollars earned by a family in a single week." [12] "When it was known that a factory was to be built, families of Poor Whites in great numbers came to the site to engage jobs . . . in advance. Almost in every case a village had to be erected to receive them. In some instances they actually stood about, waiting for the clapboards to be nailed to the studding." [13] The North also had its poor whites, eagerly searching for work, but most of them came from the farms of Quebec, Ireland, and the Continent rather than from the surrounding countryside.

Once settled in their new homes, such families set out to earn money as fast as they could. Into their shacks and tenement rooms they crowded as many boarders as they could accommodate. Boys and girls went to the mills, regardless of the law, as soon as the mills would have them. Older children took jobs as a matter of course. Thus, through the combined efforts of every member, many families succeeded in earning $25 a week—not only more than they had dreamed of, but more than most families of skilled workers and small tradesmen had to live on.

The cities of 1890 were populated largely by families such as these and by others which shared, in less extreme form, the same kind of background and ambition. The enormous expansion of the urban population after the Civil War was a reflection not so much of natural increase as of migration from farm to city and of immigration from Europe. During the three decades after the beginning of the war, the rural population declined from 80 to 65 percent of the total, and the flow into the city from the farm was small compared to the flow from Europe. In New York,

Chicago, San Francisco, Detroit, and Cleveland, for instance, three fourths of the population were immigrants or the children of immigrants. Many of the immigrants came from impoverished rural communities, and most of them came to find better jobs and make more money.

For many girls who were born and brought up in the city, the choice between staying home and taking a job was not so simple. They and their families were also caught up in the ceaseless striving to improve one's position that has always been the special distinction of American life. In all likelihood, however, the family of the urban-bred girl had already made considerable progress. Most native-born, white, English-speaking urban men were skilled, white-collar, or professional workers, and at this level the desire for more money came into sharp conflict with the conviction of polite society that a gentlewoman's place was in the home. This was a real and serious consideration. When U.S. Commissioner of Labor Carroll D. Wright reviewed the difficulties of the urban working woman in 1888, he found that her low social standing was one of her greatest problems. He thought it necessary to call upon the churches to welcome her, and urged parents to teach their children that "the honest working woman is entitled to the respect of all honest-minded people." [14]

Middle- and upper-class prejudice against paid employment for women was reenforced by the scarcity of jobs suitable for the daughters of families that had begun to climb the social and economic ladder. When the father had advanced to the pay and status of craftsman or white-collar worker, when the family had moved into a comfortable flat or into its own home in a pleasant neighborhood, a daughter could not be permitted to suffer the drudgery, dirt, noise, and even danger of unskilled factory work. Nor could she be allowed to associate with the uncouth immigrants who worked in factories. Domestic service, of course, was out of the question. A generation, or even a decade, earlier, these considerations would have eliminated all but two options: the young woman could teach school or stay home. By 1890, however, there was a rising demand for women in a variety of white-collar jobs which were free of many of the drawbacks of factory and domestic work. The daughter might take a job, for instance, as salesgirl, clerical worker, telephone operator, or typist. Teaching and nursing were also growing rapidly, and the necessary qualifications for each were well within the reach of the daughters of the lower middle class.

Oddly enough, many girls were well prepared for the new jobs that were opening up precisely because they had been expected to stay home and help their mothers. Since girls could help their mothers after school, many were allowed to complete high school. Their brothers, however, were expected to go to work rather than to high school unless they were among the few who were aiming at professional careers. Consequently, twice as many girls as boys graduated from the nation's public high schools in 1890.[15] Many of the girls were delighted to find that with little or no additional preparation they were welcomed in a variety of white-collar occupations.

Most of these girls came from the lower middle class. Of all the important occupations open to women in 1890, teaching enjoyed the highest status and prestige. According to a study conducted in 1911, however, the father of the average young woman teacher earned only $800 a year—a figure which suggests that women teachers were usually the daughters of skilled or clerical workers, or of moderately prosperous farmers.[16] Volunteer work was still the only way for the daughter of a professional or businessman to engage in responsible activities outside the home without sacrificing her social standing.

While girls from poorer families were usually better educated than their brothers, the reverse was true in upperclass families. Very few women prepared for professional work by going to college. A college education was not yet widely accepted as a mark of social standing for young women, nor even as an acceptable way of filling the years between high school and marriage. On the contrary, it was often viewed as evidence of strongminded and unfeminine disregard for social convention. In 1891 one observer reviewed the progress of college education for women in the South. A woman who approved of equal educational opportunities for women, the most she could say was that "there are women college graduates here and there, and it is no longer necessary to look upon them as monstrosities." [17] Although attitudes were more liberal in other regions, only 2,700 women graduated from college in 1890. Twice as many girls as boys were graduating from public high schools, but five times as many men were graduating from college.[18]

The few young women who did prepare for professional careers other than teaching and nursing were distinguished by their disrespect for convention and determination to override all obstacles. If not active feminists, they were often deeply affected by the feminist revolt. Many of them could see no hope of freedom in marriage, and remained single. More than one fourth of the women who graduated from college around the turn of the century never married. Of those who went on to establish professional careers, even fewer married. More than half the women doctors in 1890 were single. About one fifth were widowed or divorced, and only about one fourth were married.

Most of the married women who worked outside the home had little choice; they were the victims of one misfortune or another which deprived them of adequate support by a husband. The kinds of adversities which led wives to seek work are suggested by a study conducted by the U.S. Bureau of Labor Statistics in 1908. Among one group of 140 wives and widows who were employed in the glass industry, 94 were widows, or had been deserted, or were married to men who were permanently disabled. Thirteen were married to drunkards or loafers who would not work. The husbands of ten were temporarily unable to work because of sickness or injury. Seventeen were married to unskilled laborers who received minimum wages for uncertain employment. Only six were married to regularly employed workers above the grade of unskilled labor.[19]

Such troubles were frequent in nineteenth-century America, and since society made little organized effort to help the unfortunate, they usually had to fend for themselves. If they possibly could, they were surely better off fending for themselves. Aid was available only as charity, which was reserved for paupers, and was still influenced by the philosophy that the way to control pauperism was to keep its victims as miserable as possible. The only help a widowed mother was likely to get from public or private charity was an offer to place her children in an orphanage. The

states did not begin to provide public assistance to widowed
or abandoned mothers of young children until the decade
before World War I.[20]

⎛ The death of the husband was the most common emergency which forced married women to seek work. Pneumonia and tuberculosis were still formidable killers, and the
large cities still suffered periodic outbreaks of typhus, ty-
phoid fever, and smallpox.[21] Precautions against industrial
accidents and poisons were rudimentary. Around 1900 railroad trainmen were killed at the rate of nearly one percent
a year; coal miners at the rate of one percent every two
years.[22] Pain, paralysis, and eventual slow death from lead
poisoning awaited house painters and employees of the
nonferrous ore processing plants of the West. One out of
every five husbands was dead from these or similar causes
before he reached the age of forty-five.

Of the 2 million widows in the population, consequently,
one fourth were under forty-five years of age, and nearly
half were under fifty-five. Among these younger widows—
many of whom had children to support—more than half
were counted as gainfully occupied by the Census. The
widows of farmers were likely to stay on the farm and run
it with the help of children, neighbors, or hired hands. In
the cities, on the other hand, the great majority of working
widows were employed as housekeepers, laundresses, servants, charwomen, and in other service occupations. Suddenly and desperately in need of work, usually without
skills except those they had learned in keeping house,
widows were often forced to take the lowest paid, most demanding, and least desired jobs.

One young widow with three children worked seventy-
five hours a week in a cotton mill in Cleveland County,

North Carolina, in 1891. Her wages were $2.40 per week, but, because of sickness and layoffs, she earned only $85 during the year. Her two older children, a boy and a girl aged twelve and nine, also worked seventy-five hours a week in the mill. Their wages, $1.50 each per week, brought the family's income for the year up to $150. "I am not able to send my children to school," the mother wrote to the state Commissioner of Labor Statistics. "I have to work and have them work. This is a cause of grief to me, as they are bright children, and would be smart in books if they had a chance. I will do my best for them, and I daily ask God to help me discharge my duty to them." [23]

Even if a widow was in easier circumstances, her position in the community was awkward. In recalling the death of her father from a chronic ailment which the doctors could neither diagnose nor treat, Mary Austin wrote with bitter sympathy of her mother's humiliation.

At that time . . . the status of Wife and Mother, always spoken of in capitals, was sentimentally precious. . . . No matter how poorly, through incompetence, neglect, or misfortune, her husband "protected" her, she was allowed the airs and graces of a woman apart. . . . Then the blow fell and the treasured Wife became the poor Widow, the object of family bounty, not infrequently grudged, the grateful recipient of left-overs, the half-menial helper in the households of women whose husbands had simply not died. The more precious and delicate her wifehood had been, the less chance there was of her being equipped for earning a livelihood.

Though surrounded by friends and relatives, Mary's mother was too independent to rely on them. Equipped with fifteen years of experience in caring for seven children and an invalid husband, she "went out nursing," leaving Mary, herself a schoolgirl, to care for the youngest of the children.[24]

The same circumstances which produced so many young widows left other women with permanently or temporarily disabled husbands. In the state of Illinois alone, 15,000 husbands were disabled by industrial accidents between the middle of 1907 and the end of 1912.[25] Other wives worked because their husbands refused to provide for their families. There is no reason to think that husbands abandoned their duties more often than today, but the woman who was burdened by an irresponsible husband in 1890 usually had no recourse save taking on his responsibilities herself. If he deserted, the law-enforcement agencies of the time afforded little chance of finding and compelling him to provide support. In one department of a large South Carolina cotton mill, according to Marie Van Vorst, every worker was a grass widow. Those who had no one with whom to leave their babies brought them to the mill, where they crawled about among the machines while their mothers worked.[26] If, on the other hand, the husband stayed with his family but spent his time and money on gambling or drink, convention demanded that the wife stand by him, for better or for worse, bear his children, and, if necessary, support them as well.

Unemployment was another emergency which forced some married women to work. In most years, when business conditions were good, few husbands were unemployed for very long. On the other hand, even brief unemployment could bring serious financial difficulty, and most workers— and nearly all of the unskilled workers who could least afford to be without work—were laid off from time to time. Most construction work stopped entirely during the winter months in the North. Steel and iron furnaces closed down regularly for two months each summer for repairs. Coal mining, clothing manufacture, food processing, and many other industries were also highly seasonal. In coal-mining towns and other communities where the one major industry was seasonal, unemployment hit almost every family every year. The only way a man could escape was to take up another occupation somewhere else. According to a Bureau of Labor Statistics study of 25,000 working-class families, half of the principal breadwinners were unemployed during some part of the year 1901, and the unemployed lost an average of over two months of work.[27] When business conditions were not good, prolonged unemployment was even more widespread. During the five depression years from 1893 to 1898, unemployment in the manufacturing and transportation industries ranged from two to three times as high as before the panic of 1893, and thousands of men were without work for months at a time.[28]

Even during a severe depression, there was little public relief for the unemployed, and private charity could not begin to meet their needs. When a family ran out of savings, it resorted to the pawnshop, credit from the grocer and landlord, and borrowing from friends and relatives. The children might leave school to take work, and frequently the mother too sought employment. Even in depression years the chronic shortage of servants made it possible for women to find temporary work doing laundry, or cleaning, or other day work in private homes. And, particularly in the garment industry, there were always employers willing to hire a woman for less than the going wage.

Around the turn of the century, in short, when a married woman worked it was usually a sign that something had gone wrong. Even among the families of unskilled workers in the most miserable slum districts of the great cities, few women worked regularly if they were married to men who were able and willing to work. Just before the depression began in 1893, the Bureau of Labor interviewed every family living in some of the worst slum districts of New York City, Baltimore, Chicago, and Philadelphia. Only in New York were as many as 5 percent of the wives employed, and in Chicago only 2 percent were at work.[29]

There were only two large groups of people in the United States among whom it was not at all unusual for women to work regularly for most of their lives. The largest of these groups were the Negroes, the great majority of whom still lived in the South. According to the Census, nearly one fourth of all Negro wives, and nearly two thirds of the large number of Negro widows, were gainfully occupied. It goes without saying that Negro wives worked largely because their wages were essential to the support of their families. Sixty percent of all Negro men worked on the poorest farms in the country, and the remaining forty percent were concentrated in the least desirable nonfarm jobs. Handicapped by ignorance, lack of skill, lack of capital, and racial barriers, few Negro men could earn enough to lift their families out of poverty.

Negro wives worked, not only because most Negro men earned very little, but also because the whole pattern of their family life was different. Under slavery, of course, men and women alike did whatever work was required of them, and even when parents and children remained together, the slave father had no responsibility for support. In 1890, only twenty-five years after the Civil War, the imprint of generations of slavery was still plain. Among the poorest of the former field slaves and their descendants, men and women often came together, had children, and drifted into new partnerships as fancy dictated. The woman was often the center of the family. By working, as she always had, as a servant, a laundress, a field hand, she provided food and shelter for her children. Frequently the grandmother or some other female relative cared for the children while the mother worked. Sometimes the father of her children had disappeared; sometimes there was a series of fathers. As time passed, a growing majority of Negro families conformed more closely to the conventional pattern of family life in America. But even where this was true, much of the status and responsibility which fell to the male head of the white family was shared by the wife in the Negro family.

The immigrant wives who worked in the spinning and weaving rooms of the New England textile mills constituted the only other large group of regularly employed married women. In the Massachusetts towns of Fall River and Lowell, nearly one fifth of the married women worked, the great majority of them in the textile mills. Almost all of these women were immigrants, or daughters of immigrants, most of them from French Canada or Ireland. Some of the reasons why so many of them worked are plain. Spinning and weaving were, by long tradition, women's tasks. The work was light and easily learned. Since many of the older children worked in the mills, their mothers were not needed at home to care for them. Indeed, a mother whose children worked could look after them better if she went to work in the same mill.

Although men's wages for unskilled work in the textile mills were lower than in any other manufacturing industry, the New England textile families were no poorer than the families of most other industrial workers. The French Canadian fathers who worked in the Massachusetts cotton mills in 1892 earned an average of less than $400 a year. The total income from the work of fathers, mothers, and children, however, was over $800 a year. Of seventy-one such families interviewed by the U.S. Bureau of Labor, twenty-two were earning over $1,000 a year at a time when the annual wages of the average skilled craftsman came to about $600 or $700.[30] Many of the wives who worked in the mills did so for the same reason that led them to send sons and daughters to work. To people who had never before experienced the advantage of having money, the lure of regular wages was often irresistible.

In addition to the few large, readily identified groups of employed married women, there were a few thousand other wives who defied convention by going to work even though they did not have to support themselves or dependents. Some of them were professional women—doctors, lawyers, teachers—whose husbands did not object to their wives having a career. Some were factory workers, especially in the garment, shoe, and tobacco industries. Many of these were young, recently married women, working only until they became pregnant. Some, however, were women who had long been married but were impervious to the insistent demand of the community that they stay home.

Today, all types of women work—the young and the old, the rich and the poor, the married and the single, the illiterate and the college-educated. Only two large categories of women are not well represented in the nation's labor force—young mothers of preschool children, and women above sixty-five.

Although it is now unusual for a young, single woman not to work once she leaves school, single women account for only about one fourth of the total number of working women. The reason for this is simply that there are so few single women who are not in school. As school attendance has been prolonged, and as the age of marriage has fallen in recent years, more and more young women have been getting married shortly after leaving school, if not before.

This development in itself is one of the reasons why marriage no longer ends the working lives of women. In 1890 women were likely to spend most of their married lives bearing and rearing children. Especially among the urban middle classes, marriage was often postponed until the prospective husband was able to support a family in appropriate style, and many brides were in their late twenties or even older. Among the poorer groups in the population, and in the country, women usually got an earlier start on motherhood, but they had many more children. By the time the last of her children went off to school, the average mother was forty, and many were approaching fifty, with only two more decades of life ahead of them.

Today, on the other hand, the whole process of courtship, engagement, marriage, and motherhood has been speeded up. With dating and going steady beginning in junior high school or before, most girls are married in their late teens or very early twenties. According to one estimate, the average mother now has the last of her two or three children when she is still in her mid-twenties. When she is little past thirty, she finds herself, healthy, vigorous, and active, with no children to look after for most of the day.[31] Because of this as well as improvements in health and life expectation, she still has more than forty years ahead of her—about fifteen years more than the average mother at the same stage of family life in 1890.

These changes in the life cycle of women have helped to set the stage for a revolution in the female labor force. Today, whether married or not, almost all young women go to work when they leave school, and most of them continue to work until shortly before their first child is born. Most of them then retire, but within a few years, when their children are in school, they begin to return to work. Indeed, nearly half of all mothers of school-aged children were employed for some part of the year in 1956. Of the 21 million girls and women who were working in March of that year, more than 11 million were married and living with their husbands, compared with only 5 million who were single and less than 5 million who were widowed, divorced, or separated. Of the 11 million working wives, 9 million had no children under six, and 8 million were at least thirty-five years old. Thus, older married women, once a small minority among women workers, are now the largest group.

For the most part, paid employment in 1890 was confined not only to single women, but to the minority of women who lived in towns and cities where work for women was readily available. Where a woman lives now has much less effect on her opportunities for finding work. In many parts of the country the distinctions between rural and urban have all but disappeared as people, industry, and trade have moved out from the towns and cities to form vast overlapping suburbs.[32] Urban and suburban growth, together with the mobility of the automobile age, have combined to bring a variety of employment opportunities within reach of many rural women. One eighth of the farm population of the United States now lives in counties designated as metropolitan areas by the Census Bureau, and well over half of the working women living on farms are employed in nonfarm jobs. It is still true that relatively more women work in urban than in rural areas, but this is largely a result of the concentration of young single women in cities. Among married women, about 25 percent of those who live in rural areas are now in the labor force, compared to about 30 percent of those who live in towns and cities.

Differences in the employment opportunities of women from city to city have also dwindled. Women still have a better chance of finding work in some cities than in others. There are more jobs for them in light industry towns such as Fall River or Winston-Salem, or in great commercial centers such as New York and Chicago, than in cities such as Pittsburgh, Scranton, or Toledo, which are dominated by heavy industries. State capitals, insurance centers such as Hartford, and other places where an unusual volume of paper work is performed also provide abundant jobs for women. But there is no city today with as low a proportion of working women as in Homestead, Pennsylvania in 1890. And, surprisingly enough, there is no city today with relatively as many working women as there were then in Fall River.

One reason is that there are no longer many towns or cities so completely dominated by a single industry as Homestead was dominated by iron and steel, or Fall River by textiles. In every city, moreover, there has been a vast increase in the number of jobs in schools, hospitals, stores, restaurants, offices, and other institutions which rely heavily on women workers. On the other hand, the disappearance of children from the factories has made it impossible for any community to employ as many single girls as worked in the mill towns of New England in 1890.

The relationship between the employment of women and the financial and social status of their families has also been transformed. The nation's workers now include many more women from middle- and upper-income families than in 1890, and many fewer who work so that they and their dependents may eat. The death rate for men of working age has dropped to half or less than half of the 1890 level. Because the life span of women has increased even more than that of men, there are slightly more widows today, relative to the number of women in the population, but there are far fewer widows who are young enough to work and too young to have children who are able to support them. And there are still fewer who have young children to support. More than half of all widows are sixty-five or older today, compared to less than one third in 1890.

Other misfortunes which compel women to work have also become less frequent. Never before has the nation been so long free of severe unemployment. Seasonal fluctuations in employment are much smaller than they were at the end of the last century. Because of increased regularity of employment, greater than average increases in the wages of the lowest-paid jobs, and a sharp decline in the relative number of workers in unskilled jobs, fewer families live on the borderline of poverty where any new reverse may compel a woman to go to work in order to add to the family income.[33]

While the number of women deprived of the earnings of husbands was growing smaller, society was also doing more and more to relieve the burdens of those who were hit by disaster. Public and private pension plans, public programs for the support of the aged, the disabled, and dependent children, unemployment compensation, medical insurance plans, workmen's compensation laws, accident liability insurance, and relief payments by local government are only some of the more important kinds of financial aid for families in which the husband and father is unable or unwilling to provide support. Today, moreover, it is much easier than it was in 1890 for a woman to separate from or divorce an errant husband, and still compel him to contribute to her support.

Poverty still compels some women to work. The Aid to Dependent Children program, which is partially supported by Federal funds, provides the only public assistance available to many widowed or abandoned mothers. In very few states are the payments enough to support a family. This is a result, partly of public frugality, partly of the belief that larger payments would encourage illegitimacy and desertion.[34] There were, in 1956, nearly one million mothers of children under six years of age who were widowed, divorced, deserted, or not living with their husbands for other reasons. Nearly half of them were working, compared to only about 15 percent of the mothers of preschool children who were living with their husbands.

No one knows how many of today's working women have to work, but we do know how much money they and their families have to live on. In 1956, there were about 7 million married working women whose husbands were also employed full time, the year round. The average income of these families was $6,575. Among all families of working wives—whether or not the husband was employed—nearly two out of three had total incomes over $5,000, and more than one out of three had more than $7,000.

In 1890 most middle- and upper-income families derived all their income from the work of the husband and older, unmarried sons. Today, however, many families are in the middle-income brackets only because women, too, are working. Of all families whose income ranged from $7,000 to $15,000 in 1956, 70 percent had at least two workers, and most of the supplementary earners were women. It is still true that the more a man earns, the less likely is his wife to work. Nevertheless, even in families where the husband's earnings are well above average, a great many wives work. Thus, husbands who earned between $7,000 and $10,000 in 1956 were in the upper eighth of the income scale. In these families, half of the wives who had no children at home were working early in 1957. Even among those who had school-aged children, one fourth were in the labor force.

Along with the increasing employment of women from middle- and upper-income families has come a tremendous improvement in the educational qualifications of women workers. As American women have received more and more education, those who have received the most have gone to work in largest number. Today more than half of all women college graduates are employed, compared to four out of ten high school graduates, three out of ten elementary school graduates, and only two out of ten among those with less than five grades of school. Most of the working girls of 1890 were ignorant and unskilled, but today's working women have considerably more education than women who do not work. Among those who have only recently completed school and gone to work, nearly three fourths are high school graduates, and less than 10 percent have not been to high school at all.

Most well-educated middle-class working women hold

white collar or professional jobs, which now employ more than half of all working women. Although many other kinds of work have become widely available to women, clerical work and teaching continue to provide most of the jobs for women high school and college graduates. About three fifths of the girls going to work after graduating from high school take clerical jobs, and about the same proportion of the young women going to work after college become teachers.

The high level of employment among well-educated women is related to the fact that they tend to have fewer family responsibilities than other women. As in 1890, they are more likely never to marry, or they tend to marry later and have fewer children than women with less education. During the last two decades, however, all of these tendencies have grown weaker. The proportions of women who never marry or have children is lower than ever before. The rise in the marriage and birth rates and the drop in the age at marriage have been most pronounced among the same high school and college-educated middle-class women who have also been flocking into the labor force. In 1950 seven out of ten women college graduates in their late twenties were married, compared to only half in 1940. The 1950 group, moreover, had had three times as many babies as the 1940 group. Since 1950, college women have apparently been marrying still earlier, and having even more babies. In the fall of 1956, one out of every four young people attending college was already married.

Explanations of the apparent eagerness of middle-class boys and girls to plunge into marriage and parenthood at the earliest opportunity have usually stressed the abundance of good jobs available in recent years. If this is true, it seems likely that employment opportunities for women have helped to bolster the confidence which permits people to marry earlier and have larger families. Since the beginning of World War II, it has become possible for a woman to marry and remain at work, and to have children and return to work whenever her family's needs or wants outstrip its income.

That young women today are having more babies than their mothers, if not more than their grandmothers, has not proved to be an obstacle to their return to work. Because young people are marrying and starting their families earlier than ever before, women are still young when their last child goes off to school. The increasing size of the American family may even be one of the circumstances which has contributed to the growing employment of mothers. In 1890 children were the principal source of supplementary income. The more children there are in a family today, however, the more difficult it is to meet the costs of bringing them up properly. Many mothers have apparently concluded that they can do more for their families by working for a pay envelope than by staying at home.

The increasing employment of middle-class, middle-aged wives is but one aspect of a series of developments that have tended to eliminate sharp differences in American society. The alien character of the city and of the industrial labor force has been diluted by the curtailment of new immigration, by the assimilation of the children of the older immigrants, and by the steady inflow of the native-born from the farms. Rural and urban ways of life have come closer together. Many local and regional peculiarities have been all but erased as a result of increased mobility, improved communication, and spreading industrialization. The vast gulf between the very rich and the very poor has been narrowed. Status distinctions among occupation have been blurred as the wages of manual labor have risen, and the brutalizing aspects of manual work in the last century have been abolished. The spread of free public education has reduced the cultural and economic advantages of the well-born. For present purposes, at least, the most important of the fading contrasts in American life is the contrast between the activities of men and women. Going to work is only one among a host of activities—ranging from smoking cigarettes and wearing pants to voting and going to college—which were formerly reserved for men, but are now shared by women.

Of all large groups of Americans, the Negroes remain the most isolated. Inescapably marked by color, handicapped by segregated and inadequate schools, living apart from the white community, Negro workers are still concentrated in the lowest-paid, least desirable jobs. As in 1890 the low earnings of Negro men reenforce the matriarchal tendency of Negro family life, and Negro women are much more likely to work than white women. Yet the differences separating white and Negro have also diminished over the last half century, and especially over the last twenty years. Negroes have been moving in large numbers from farm to city, and from South to North and West, and by moving they have improved their opportunities for both education and employment.[35]

Progress toward assimilation of the Negro population is reflected in the slowly diminishing differences between the employment patterns of white and Negro women. In 1890 the proportion employed was at least twice as high for Negro as for white women, but the margin has now been reduced to about one third. The narrowing of this difference is partly a reflection of the fact that rising income among Negroes has made it possible for young girls and elderly women to withdraw from the labor force. Mainly, however, it reflects the fact that employment of middle-aged married women has been rising much more rapidly among whites than among Negroes.

The circumstances which determine whether or not a woman works have changed enormously since 1890. Fewer women are forced to work by poverty. On the other hand, the conventions which once prevented most women from seeking employment have all but disappeared. Like their brothers, single women are now expected to work, no matter what the circumstances of their families. The choice between job and home now falls mainly to wives and mothers, who rarely worked in 1890 unless they had to. Once her children are in school, the modern mother has more freedom of choice than the single woman had in 1890. Her decision is less dependent on where she lives, the social and economic status of her family, the color of her skin, or where her parents were born; more dependent on her own desires and the changing needs of her family.

Chapter III

THE DEMANDS
AND REWARDS OF
WOMEN'S WORK

BEFORE the turn of the century, the relationship between workers and employers was often very casual. The employer wanted hands who would do their work and obey his rules for as long as he needed them. He was not expected to take responsibility for their welfare, and few businessmen were aware of the possibility of increasing profits through careful attention to the management of people. Procedures for hiring, firing, assigning, training, and promoting employees were highly informal, and most employers gave little thought to the morale of their workers or the conditions of their work.

The employment relationship was even more casual for women workers than for men. Since most working women had little skill or training, they were easily replaced. A woman might be fired if she violated a petty work rule, if she became ill and stayed home for a few days, or when the busy season ended. On the other hand, most employed women were not entirely dependent on their own wages, and many of them were young girls exploring the world of work to see if they could find a place that suited them.

A girl might quit if she took a dislike to a supervisor or fellow worker, if she heard of a better job, or if she wanted some time off. Unless she lived in a one-company town, or unless it was a depression year, she knew that she could always get another job about as good. The fragile link between women workers and their employers was illustrated during an investigation of the garment industry conducted in 1895 by a committee of the New York legislature. Even in small shops, many girls knew their employers only by sight, not by name, and many employers did not even have records of their employee's names.[1]

The usual way to get an industrial job around the turn of the century was to walk into a factory and ask for work. When Marie Van Vorst arrived in Lynn, Massachusetts, in 1901, she entered one of the largest shoe factories, found a forewoman, and asked for a beginner's job. The forewoman, wrote Miss Van Vorst,

didn't even look at me, but called . . . above the machine din . . . : "Got anything for a green hand?" The person addressed gave me one glance, the sole . . . look I got from anyone in authority . . . "Ever worked in a shoe-shop before?"
"No ma'am."
"I'll have you learned pressin'; we need a presser."

After two and a half hours in town, she was at work. A few weeks later, in Columbia, South Carolina, she went into the largest spinning mill in the world, found an overseer, and asked for work. She was told to wander around, pick out a standing or sitting job, and to report for work that afternoon.[2]

While Miss Van Vorst was posing as a working woman, Dorothy Richardson, a young orphan from rural Pennsylvania, was looking for work in New York City. She had been a country schoolteacher, and spent several fruitless weeks looking for a genteel job. With funds running low, she set out one morning, resolved to take the best job she could find. Relying on newspaper ads, signs on doorways, and random inquiries, she was turned down at two cigar factories for lack of experience, and then refused an offer to become an apprentice cigar maker with a promise of $5 a week after three years. Giving up the cigar industry, she accepted a job as a learner in a book bindery at $3, but kept on looking. A small storekeeper offered her $3.50 for an 87-hour week. She was refused, again for lack of experience, at a candy factory. She turned down a job at $1.50 as a learner in an artificial flower sweatshop, and finally accepted $3 at a paper box factory.

Leaving this job after several weeks, over a disagreement with a fellow worker, she responded to a doorway sign and got a job making artificial flowers at $3.50. She was well pleased with the job, but after four weeks was laid off because the flower-hat season was over. The next day, she and two other flower makers answered a newspaper advertisement, and all three were hired to operate power sewing machines at piece rates in a ladies' underwear factory. Together they made less than ten cents during the first half day, so one of them quit immediately to look for better jobs for all. The next day they were at work in a jewel box shop, earning $3 for only 47 hours a week, compared to the 60 hours they were accustomed to. Miss Richardson lost this job when she took three days off to attend to urgent personal affairs.

Walking the streets again, and needing work immediately, she saw a sign "Shakers wanted—Apply to Foreman."

I didn't know what a "shaker" was, but that didn't deter me. I . . . filed up the stairs with a crowd of other girls. . . . At the head of the stairs we filed into a mammoth, steam-filled room. . . . The foreman made quick work of us. . . . At last it came my turn.

"Hello, Sally! Ever shook?"

"No."

"Ever work in a laundry?"

"No; but I'm very handy." . . .

"All right, Sally; we'll start you in at three and a half a week, and maybe we'll give you four dollars after you get broke in."

The foreman hired thirty-two girls in the same casual way. Many had come with a man, who, she was told, "goes out with a wagon when they run short of help, and . . . picks up any girls he can find and hauls them in."

She kept the laundry job until the owner showed an interest in her by making "some joking remarks of insulting flattery," rudely pinching her "bare arm," and offering a promotion to the wrapping department. The foreman hinted that this was a proposition, and that since she was a nice girl, she had better leave.[3]

Domestic service jobs were usually found through employment agencies, or, as they were called, "intelligence offices." An intensive study of these offices in 1902 concluded that most of them sought to extract the largest possible fee for the smallest possible service. At worst, they practiced calculated fraud.

Exploitation of both mistresses and servants was made possible by the chronic shortage of domestic help, the ignorance and poverty of many of the girls looking for work as servants, and total lack of regulation. The girls seeking work were easily victimized. Most of them were naïve farm girls. Many were Negroes from the rural South, or immigrants just off the boat, usually unable to speak English, sometimes without friends or relatives in the city. The larger agencies actively recruited and imported girls from the farms and from Europe, sometimes advancing the cost of transportation, which was later repaid with exorbitant interest.

There were many methods of fraud. Under pressure from an agency which had advanced her money, a girl might agree to take and quit a series of jobs, so that the agency could collect a fee from each employer. Or, an agency might arrange with a hotel or rooming house to hire a series of girls, each of whom paid a fee, and then fire them, sometimes without pay. Most agencies maintained rooms where girls could live until they were placed. Some would not place a girl unless she lived at the agency, and then not until she had run out of money to pay the high prices for bad food and dirty bedding that the agency charged. Some agencies were procurers for houses of prostitution, and there were not a few authenticated cases of girls looking for work who were kidnaped and forced into prostitution.[4]

Employment agencies were also widely used to place teachers, clerical workers, and nurses. These agencies were generally more reputable than domestic service agencies, but all charged high fees whether or not the applicant got a job. Many teachers' agencies charged a nonreturnable registration fee of $5, plus 10 percent of a year's salary.[5] Most teachers were hired in the same casual way as industrial workers, without benefit of employment agencies or other formalities. Any girl who had completed six or eight years of school, and had reached the age of seventeen or eighteen, could apply to the local authorities for a position. If she passed a perfunctory examination, usually given by men no better educated than she, and if she could come to terms with them on salary, she was likely to be hired. If there was no vacancy in her own district, there was sure to be one not far away. The demand for new teachers was steady, since school enrollment was growing and since few teachers stayed in their posts for long. In 1880, 37 percent of the teachers in Illinois were replaced before the end of the school year. Nearly three decades later, a survey conducted by the National Education Association found that in most states about 80 percent of the one-room rural schools opened each fall with a new teacher.[6]

Nursing still had more in common with domestic than with professional service. The usual work of nurses was to do whatever was required of them in homes where extra help was needed because someone was sick. Consequently, employment agencies for domestics often placed nurses as well as other servants. Hospital nursing was performed almost entirely by students, and even the trained nurse had few opportunities outside of private duty. Nursing schools and local nurses' associations provided registration and placement services for trained nurses, but most hospital schools did little to find positions for their graduates. The hospitals were interested in their schools of nursing mainly as a source of cheap labor, and some received a good deal of income by renting out their students for duty in private homes, ostensibly as part of their training. The first state law to protect nurses and patients by setting standards for registration and placement was not passed until 1903.[7]

The most important qualification for most of the factory jobs held by women in 1890 was the ability to perform a simple, repetitive task at sustained high speed. The women who "opened" tin plate in the sheet rolling mills, or pushed heavy trucks of wet clothing in the steam laundries, needed strong arms and backs, but most heavy labor was performed by men. Women usually worked like Sister Carrie, who sat all day on a stool and fed shoe uppers, one by one, into a machine which punched lace holes;[8] or like Mrs. John Van Vorst, who stood at a table and pressed cork linings into thousands upon thousands of pickle jar covers.[9]

Dorothy Richardson was exhausted long before the end of her first day in the paper box factory. "The awful noise and confusion, the terrific heat, the foul smell of the glue, and the agony of breaking ankles and blistered hands seemed almost unendurable," she wrote. Her first impression of a garment factory was "a very inferno of sound. . . . The girls, who sat in long rows . . . did not raise their eyes to the newcomers. . . . Every face, tense and stony, bespoke a superb effort to concentrate mind and body, and soul itself, literally upon the point of a needle." Her most tiring assignment, however, was one of the lighter jobs in a laundry, shaking and straightening out the wash as it came tangled from the wringers. The heat and humidity of the workroom were so great that even nineteenth-century modesty failed, and men and women alike were "driven to a state of half dress." For all but the first quarter hour of her first twelve-hour day as a shaker, she suffered "that excruciating, nerve-torturing pain which comes as a result of ceaseless muscular action that knows no variation or relaxation."[10]

In each of these jobs, the stress of the work itself was multiplied by other difficulties—bad smells, noise, heat, humidity. Other irksome conditions in many factories included overcrowding, poor light, dirt, and dangerous

and unhealthy processes and procedures. To some extent
these conditions simply reflected the current state of industrial technology. Men had not yet learned how to make
machines that did not clank and clatter, grease that did not
drip, metal forming processes that did not require great
heat, nor glues and dyes that did not stink. The day of the
freestanding machine, individually powered by its own
electric motor, had not yet arrived. Most machines were
powered by belts which ran from central shafts, driven, in
turn, by other belts which ran through floors and ceilings
to the boiler room in the basement. This method of con-
veying steam power had various deficiencies. It meant that
the heat of the boiler room rose through the factory. It
meant overcrowding, for machines had to be grouped as
close as possible to the central source of energy. The complex system of shafts and belts was inherently noisy and
dangerous; it cut off a good deal of the light; and it impeded
efforts to mechanize the handling of materials and to organ-
ize the flow of work so as to minimize hauling, lifting, and
carrying.[11]

The inevitable strains of work under such circumstances
were often augmented by the employer's total indifference
to the health and welfare of his workers.[12] Many factories,
especially in the garment and food industries, were overrun
with vermin. The New Jersey Bureau of Labor Statistics
reported, in 1888, that the linen thread spinners of Patterson
were "compelled to stand on a stone floor in water the year
round, most of the time barefoot, with a spray of water
from a revolving cylinder flying constantly against the
breast; and, the coldest night in winter . . . those poor
creatures must go to their homes with the water dripping
from their under-clothing . . . because there could not

be space or a few moments allowed them wherein to change. . . ." [13] The lint-filled, moisture-saturated atmosphere of the Southern cotton mills led to constant expectoration, and floors were slimy with a mixture of sputum and tobacco juice. In other industries, the atmosphere was even more dangerously contaminated by tobacco, glass, mica, or brass dust, or by the fumes of naptha, lacquer, paint, and other volatile materials. In all of these industries, tuberculosis, pneumonia, and less serious respiratory infections were common.

In the shoe industry women scrubbed the excess glue and dye from the finished product with bits of rag dipped in hot, soapy water. The water soon became a black, corrosive solution of glue, dye, and soap which stained the hands beyond cleansing, rotted the skin, and ate away the fingernails. Artificial flower makers developed horny, spade-fingered hands from constant use of hot irons to press their delicate creations to shape. Arsenic, lead, mercury, and phosphorus were used in a variety of industrial processes, usually with little or no effort to prevent poisoning. The perils of the girls who worked in match factories were described by one observer in 1903, with a curious mixture of revulsion and cheerful optimism.

The constant inhalation of phosphorus results in a terrible and deadly disease known as necrosis of the jawbone. A warning is usually mercifully given to match makers by toothache—the first symptom of the disease. Match makers often inhale so much phosphorus that their very breath shows phosphorescence in the dark, and as the evil results begin in the mouth, only persons with absolutely sound teeth are employed. Much of the evil effect of phosphorus is avoided by compelling the operatives to wear small tin boxes, containing turpentine, suspended at their necks.

After pointing out that necrosis of the upper jaw is invariably fatal, the author concluded that

strong persons in modern match factories are as safe as they would be in any factory where chemicals are used, but the weak, the scrofulous—these had better fly from phosphorus as from the plague.[14]

Wherever mechanical presses, rollers, or cutting or stamping devices were used, severed fingers and crushed hands were not unusual. Indeed, such accidents occurred wherever machines of any kind were used. Safety devices to keep hands out of danger were rarely provided, and machines were often cleaned, oiled, and adjusted while running. Whenever paper, cloth, or other inflammable materials were used, the danger of fire was constant. The New York state legislature was not convinced of the need for effective regulation of factories to prevent fires and provide escape routes until 1911, when 145 girls and women died in the Triangle Shirtwaist Factory.

A few employers made every effort to insure that working conditions were as comfortable and healthy as possible. In 1884, for instance, an English visitor described a watch factory at Waterbury, Connecticut, where most of the employees were women.

Entering at the operatives' door, we came, first, upon the dressingroom, where each workman has his ticketed hooks for coat and hat, his own ticketed towel, while the common lavatory is equal to that of an English club. . . . The walls . . . are all windows, the ceilings are high, the warming and ventilation is perfect. There is no smoke, dust, or bad air, and the operatives are comfortably seated at their respective benches.[15]

A Pittsburgh factory which employed 600 girls in 1911 was pictured with equal enthusiasm by another observer.

The workrooms were described as

clean, well-ventilated, well-constructed. The stairways are mar-
ble, and on the walls are engravings of action and battle and
plunging horses. . . . The girls are often summoned to the
auditorium at noon to hear an address by some visitor or to
sing; in this case they have an hour's recess, instead of half an
hour. [Other amenities included a] roof garden for summer
use . . . a natatorium, with schedule so arranged that . . . the
girls may . . . swim once or twice a week after hours . . .
beautifully kept dressing rooms, and a lunch room with pic-
tures on the walls and a piano in one corner.[16]

Conditions in most factories were between these ex-
tremes. Mrs. John Van Vorst was revolted and exhausted by
her first few days in most of the jobs she tried, but once she
had become used to the noises, smells, and hazards of each
new job, and had hardened her body to the particular set
of motions demanded, the work did not seem so hard. Her
first day in a pickle factory left her so exhausted that she
had to take two days of rest before she could go back, but
within a few weeks she found that she "was equal to a long
walk after ten hours in the factory." [17]

The unpleasant and dangerous features of factory work
were not a problem for the domestic servant. How hard
the servant worked depended, of course, on the individual
employer. The major complaint of domestics was not the
amount of work they had to do, but their lack of freedom
and privacy. In New York City, in the 1880's, "a maid's
working day began at 6 A.M. and didn't close until she went
to bed at night. If the mistress were entertaining guests, the
maids were required to sit up until the guests left—even
though it were midnight. Otherwise ten o'clock was the
closing hour for the house. . . ." [18] In most homes, the maid
was allowed out one evening a week, and on every other

Sunday afternoon and evening. Thus, she was usually on call for over 100 hours a week, and since her evenings out ended at 10 P.M., she was permitted only about eight hours a week away from her employer's home.

This was a work week exceeded only by private nurses, who were on duty twenty-four hours a day, seven days a week. When, after World War I, they began to ask for a twelve-hour day, they were accused of having lost the true spirit of nursing.[19] The women who were responsible for the development of professional nursing regarded their work as a crusade. Some of the early leaders were members of religious orders. Others had had experience in military nursing during the Civil War, and all were influenced by Florence Nightingale's severe precepts about discipline and service. Consequently, the training of the nurse was less a matter of education than an ordeal to weed out the unfit, to toughen the fit, and to instill obedience and devotion. Since hospitals were happy to fall in with these ideas, student nurses were perhaps the hardest working women in America. As a rule, they spent ten to twelve hours a day (or night) on ward duty, which usually involved a great deal more heavy housekeeping than direct care of patients. Classes, lectures, and studying, if any, came in off-duty time.

Before the establishment of nursing schools, most hospitals were pestholes. In the newly established schools, of which there were many in the 1890's, the principal work of the students was literally to clean up the filth. "They found dirt and disorder to be almost universal. Vermin and infection were common even in pretentious buildings. . . . Extraordinary customs and conditions existed. In one beautiful and wealthy hospital, the morgue table was used for operations. . . ."[20] The first approach to sanitary conditions in hospitals came, not because of the insistence of the medical profession, but because student nurses were willing to work as charwomen and laundresses. One of their common duties was to wash bandages for re-use, since hospital administrators were often unable or unwilling to pay for fresh ones.

By comparison with the nurse, the urban teacher enjoyed excellent working conditions, short hours, and, with respect to physical strains, easy work. By this time most city schools were organized in classes by grades, and school buildings and supplies were more or less adequate. But the one-room school still prevailed in rural areas, with students of all ages studying together. As late as 1910, 80 percent of the nation's school buildings had one room and one teacher.[21] The typical rural school building was a one-room frame or log structure, frequently with rough hewn board floor, greased paper windows, slab seats, and a fireplace. Books and even paper were often scarce, and sometimes every student studied from a different text.

The rural teacher's principal problem was likely to be the maintenance of discipline. By long tradition the rural schoolroom was the scene of a running war between teacher and boys, especially the older ones. No new teacher could begin to teach until she had first established her authority—a task which often required a firm will and a strong arm, for a boy could not easily hold the respect of his fellows unless he received an occasional well-deserved caning. Few women could preserve their authority unless backed by the still stronger arms of their pupils' fathers, and many a teacher was driven in tears from the classroom and the profession when the men of the community failed to support her.[22]

In 1893 a young woman from a Midwestern city applied

for a position in a frontier school twenty miles from the nearest town. Although she had been recommended by a friend, the former teacher, she was surprised when she was accepted, since, as she later wrote, "I was barely sixteen, and wore short skirts, and a braid down my back. . . . I did not know until afterwards that my friend and her predecessor had both been 'run out' of this school, which consisted of about six little girls under ten years of age, and twenty rough and tumble boys ranging from twelve to nineteen." She avoided the fate of her predecessors by teaching the boys how to play baseball, on condition that they behave themselves.[23]

Office work has changed less than most other kinds of women's work. The 1890 office did not look much like the office of today. The new clerk, bookkeeper, or typist was likely to be the only woman in sight. Offices "were filled . . . with men, many of them wearing their hats indoors and spitting into . . . cuspidors which stood on rubber mats. . . . Offices almost never had rugs, and the air, which was changed as seldom as possible, smelled of cigar smoke. . . . The dominant . . . idea was to get in as much oak as possible in the form of railings and paneling and to keep everything good and dark so it wouldn't matter how much dirt accumulated."[24] Office work, however, involved little of the physical strains found in most other women's jobs. Hours were usually shorter, sometimes much shorter, than in most other work.

Women who worked in offices came to their jobs with better preparation than women in most other occupations. Except for the very few women in the learned professions, typists and stenographers were about the only working women who had usually received systematic vocational instruction. The first typing school was opened by the New York City YWCA in 1881. From then on, high school, plus a course in typing and shorthand, was the standard route into the business world for young women. By contrast, as we have seen, few teachers had any pedagogical training, and most of them had not even been to high school. As for nurses, their training in many hospitals was still limited to whatever they could pick up from the overworked second-year students who served as head nurses, and from an occasional lecture given by whatever doctor happened to be available, on whatever subject he happened to choose.

In industry women acquired their skills after they went to work. Even in industries like printing, where a great many women were employed, and where apprenticeship was widespread, women were rarely accepted as apprentices. Industrial training for women usually consisted of a few moments introduction to the job by another worker, or perhaps the foreman. Sister Carrie's experience was typical. The foreman in the shoe factory led her to another girl.

"You," he said, "show this girl how to do what you're doing. . . ."

The girl so addressed rose promptly. . . .

"It isn't hard to do," she said. . . . "You just take this so, fasten it with this clamp, and start the machine."

She . . . fastened the piece of leather . . . and pushed a small steel rod at the side of the machine. . . . After observing a few times, the girl let her work at it alone. Seeing that it was fairly well done, she went away.[25]

Dorothy Richardson's introduction to the much more difficult task of operating a power sewing machine was even more perfunctory. The foreman showed her how to thread the needle and turn the power on and off, and then left her to her own devices.[26] Mrs. John Van Vorst was more fortunate when she began work in a Chicago garment factory. She was placed under the tutelage of a tailor and a seamstress, who communicated with her and each other through signs, since one spoke only Polish and the other only German.[27]

This casual attitude toward industrial training was not peculiar to women's work. Except for the few who completed apprenticeship, men fared no better. Both sexes acquired skills as best they could as they went along. The major difference was that most women never got jobs in which they could add substantially to their skills. There were some exceptions—fields of women's work in which there was a progression of skill, promotion, and pay. In the women's coat and suit industry, a girl might eventually become a cutter. In the artificial flower shops, she might progress from making daisies to making roses. In the department stores the normal steps were cash girl, stock girl, selling in the basement, and eventually selling on one of the upper floors. In most fields, however, few steps were open to women. In any case, not many women stayed long enough in any one area to work to acquire much skill. At the end of the six or eight years that most women workers spent at work, they were likely to be performing tasks much like those they had learned on their first day.

A worker's reaction to a job depends at least as much on personal relationships with fellow workers, supervisors, and employers as it does on the work itself and on the physical surroundings of the job. The employee in 1890 spent a good deal more time in the company of fellow workers than today's worker does. Ten hours a day were usually spent on the job, in a small area crowded with other workers. Because travel was slow and difficult, working companions were often neighbors as well. And because so many workers were comparative strangers in the community, work acquaintances often formed the basis of social activities outside the factory.

Opportunities to widen one's circle of friends and acquaintances, to talk and joke with companions of one's own age and interests, perhaps even to find a suitor were among the strongest attractions which drew young women to work. This was especially true of girls who came to the factory from isolated farms. At the same time, however, ten hours of demanding work in close quarters often led to short tempers and bitter quarrels.

Relations between workers and management were shaped largely by the absence of any effective restraint on the power of the employer. What little labor legislation had been passed was rarely enforced, and very few women belonged to unions. In most shops, the boss could be as arbitrary, as domineering, as unreasonable as he pleased, and the worker's only recourse was to quit. Power over subordinates was widely delegated, and in some plants every foreman was ruler of his own empire, with complete authority to hire and fire, impose discipline, and even, within limits, to set wages. If he chose to fine a girl half a day's pay for being ten minutes late or spoiling ten cents worth of material, he did. An account in the New York *Tribune* in the mid-1880's told of a girl, whose mother had just died, who was fired from her job as a department store sales clerk for not smiling enough.[28]

The power of the employer did not always stop at the

end of the work day. Company-owned towns were rapidly disappearing in the North, but they were still common in the Pennsylvania coal fields and the Southern textile industry. In order to live in the town, the worker had not only to accept the employer's discipline at work, but also to buy in his store, live in one of his houses, and submit to his law.[29] Even if the employer did not own the town, he might seek to control his employees' actions away from work. During the anthracite coal strike in 1902, George Baer, president of the Philadelphia and Reading Coal and Iron Company, declared that "the rights and interests of the laboring man will be protected and cared for, not by the labor agitators, but by the Christian men to whom God in His infinite wisdom has given control of the property interests of the country." [30] Many employers agreed with Baer, and believed that they had the wisdom and the right to regulate their employee's lives. Drinking (even if not to excess), philandering, and even lack of thrift were sometimes viewed as grounds for dismissal. In 1905 a Chicago bank posted a notice declaring that "employees receiving a salary of less than one thousand dollars a year must not marry without first consulting the banking officials and obtaining their approval." [31] Most employers, however, were as indifferent to the welfare of their employees off the job as on. It was only the rare employer who ran a "model factory," carefully designed and maintained to protect the health and welfare of his workers, who was also likely to insist that they take good care of themselves off the job.

One such paternalistic employer was the Willimantic (Connecticut) Thread Company, which, in the middle 1880's, operated a spacious, clean, glass-roofed, flower-planted mill; an attractive, land-scaped mill village; and, among other amenities, a library for the use of employees. On the job female workers wore a uniform, and employees were expected to keep their cottages and gardens up to the high standards of the mill. The company employed a "mission-woman" whose functions included visiting the sick, counseling the troubled, and "taking shrewd note of the condition of every house she enters, reporting her daily work to the president." The manager of the mill lived in the mill village, because, as he said, "I dare as soon desert my flag in action as leave my hands without their natural and appointed head." [32]

Meddlesome interest in employees was more common outside of industrial and commercial employment. It was, perhaps, the chief complaint of domestic servants and teachers. Both in and out of school, the teacher was expected to serve as a model of perfect rectitude for her pupils. In many communities, a teacher did not dare go to a theater, dance, or play cards, much less smoke or drink. (Instruction in the evils of tobacco and alcohol was a standard part of the curriculum in some states.) Teachers were expected to read only the "right" books, and keep company, in the most decorous way, with only the right young men, and they could never afford to miss church on Sundays. In large cities, the teacher could enjoy a good deal of privacy, but in rural areas there was no way for her to escape the constant scrutiny of the community.[33]

Women's relationships with supervisors and other workers were also strongly affected by the fact that they were women while most supervisors and many co-workers were men. Many Americans had a strong suspicion that any woman who chose to work had forfeited her claim to gentle treatment, a suspicion which was reenforced by the rowdy behavior of some working women. Since they were drawn, for the most part, from the lower economic levels and frequently came from backgrounds of rural poverty, many were rough, tough, ignorant girls, who swore, chewed, stole, told vulgar stories, settled their differences in hand-to-hand combat, and followed a moral code that was far from strict.

The low esteem in which working women were held was manifested in many ways. Women were sometimes required to finish their week's work by getting down on their knees to scrub the factory floor, a task which most men would not perform. When Dorothy Richardson asked why no white men worked in the laundry, she was told that the work was fit only for "wimmin" and "naygurs." [34] In the employment agencies for domestics, women were often herded like cattle, bullied, insulted, and cheated. Indeed, in every large city there were many employers whose profits depended on systematic cheating of female employees. The Working Woman's Protective Union, founded in New York City in 1868 to provide women "with legal protection against the frauds and impositions of unscrupulous employers," had its counterpart in most other cities. Between 1868 and 1890 the New York agency collected through the courts a total of $41,000 for 12,000 women "who would otherwise have been defrauded of their hard-earned wages." [35]

Disrespect for the working girl sometimes led to sexual advances by supervisors or male workers. Girls complained of stolen embraces, pinches, and vulgar remarks. It was widely believed that many prostitutes were former working girls, first corrupted by supervisors who had threatened to fire or promised to promote them. Public concern over the moral conditions of women's employment led to an official investigation by the U.S. Bureau of Labor in 1887. The Bureau interviewed 3,866 prostitutes and found that 32 percent of them had never worked in any other occupation, while 30 percent had worked only as domestics. The report concluded that the girls who worked in factories and stores could not "be burdened with the charge of furnishing the chief source whence the ranks of prostitution are recruited. . . . The working women of the country are as honest and as virtuous as any class of our citizens. . . . They are not corrupted by their employers, nor do their employers seek to corrupt them." [36] Nevertheless, whatever lesser breaches of propriety did occur were likely to be taken very seriously by any girl who shared the extreme sensitivity of polite society toward questions of sex. Several students of women's working conditions found that it was not unusual for women who worked in mixed company to become ill rather than ask a male supervisor for permission to leave the floor, or allow male eyes to see them entering the lavatory.[37]

For her sixty hours of work, the average factory girl earned between $5 and $6 a week, or between nine and ten cents an hour.[38] Wages were lowest in the South, highest in the Far West. In the Northeast, where most factory employees lived, girls of fourteen and fifteen often started work for as little as $1.50 a week. An older girl might get $3 or possibly $4 when she started to work. If she had any competence at all, she was usually earning between $5 and $6 before very long. But in most industries, few girls ever got much beyond $8, about as much as men were usually paid for unskilled manual labor. There were exceptions, however. In the garment and shoe industries, for instance, where many operatives were paid at piece rates, a hard-working girl with years of experience at the same task might become fast enough to reach $10 or even $12.

Wages in other women's jobs were seldom much higher. In the large cities of the Northeast, wages for domestic servants who lived in usually ran from $2 to $5 a week for a work week more than half again as long as in the factory. In addition, of course, they received room and board, which was worth another $2 to $4 a week. In the department stores the pay structure was about the same as in factories, ranging, with few exceptions, from $1.50 to $8 a week. The code of fair practices which the New York Consumers' League sought to impose during the 1890's set a minimum of $2 for cash girls and $6 for experienced saleswomen.[39] Typists and stenographers fared somewhat better. Wages usually started at $6 for beginners, and ran up to $15 for capable, experienced girls.

Like servants, hospital nurses lived in and received room and board in addition to wages. Student nurses were paid on a sliding scale, starting, according to one report, at $1 a week, and rising to $4 by the end of their two years of service and training. The few who stayed on in supervisory positions got a little more. The annual salary of the superintendent of nurses in one large hospital in the 1880's was $480. Because they were in such demand, however, graduate nurses in private practice earned more than women in any other occupation. During the 1890's, $15 was the standard fee for seven days of twenty-four-hour duty, a price that only the well-to-do could afford. By 1900 some nurses were charging $25.[40]

Women workers were usually paid much less than men.

In factories they probably earned, on the average, about half as much. Concentrated in the unskilled jobs in the industries with the lowest wage scales, women frequently received less than men even when they performed roughly comparable work. The U.S. Bureau of Labor reviewed the payroll records of more than 1,000 employers and nearly 150,000 employees in 1895 and 1896, and found only 800 instances where men and women were employed in the same job classification by the same employer. In 600 of these instances, men's wages were higher than women's, by an average of about one third.[41] Inequalities in pay were most flagrant in teaching. As has been seen, teachers' salaries were fixed, not by formal schedules, but by individual bargaining between the teacher and the local school authorities. In most rural areas the outcome was little more successful for men than for women, and the usual salary for both was about $10 a week. In the cities, however, better jobs were available to men but not often to women. According to one estimate, male teachers in urban schools averaged $33 a week in 1890, compared to $13 for women.[42]

Most working women lived at home with families that received most of their income from other sources. To the average working girl a job meant that she and her family had more than before she worked, however little she earned. But what of the working girl who lived alone and had to support herself on $5 or $6 a week? In most communities barely adequate food and lodging cost her at least $2. In the New England textile towns, for instance, $2.25 per week was the usual rate for room, board, and light laundry in the austere rooming houses operated under contract to the mills during the 1880's and 1890's.[43] Shortly after 1900, Dorothy Richardson managed to live on less than $2 a week in New York City. Thus, even when she was earning less than $4, she was able to save enough to tide her over between jobs. For this sum, however, she got only a dormitory bed, and nearly inedible food.[44]

For $3 to $4, a girl could obtain comfortable lodging and fairly good meals in most communities. Marie Van Vorst paid $3.35 a week in Lynn, Massachusetts, for room and board in a private house which contained nine other boarders. She had a small attic room to herself, clean and pleasant, with papered walls; the use of an attractive, well-furnished living room; and as much food as she could eat. On her first day, dinner consisted of Irish stew, cheese, preserves, pickles, cake, and tea. Breakfast the next morning was codfish balls, bread, butter, and coffee.

The earnings and expenses of nearly 6,000 urban working women were recorded by the U.S. Bureau of Labor during its 1887 survey. Most of them lived at home but paid their parents for room and board. Their average weekly income was slightly under $6, of which a little more than $3 was spent for food and housing. Another $1.50 a week went for clothing, more than enough, at 1890 prices, to provide respectable dress for all seasons and occasions. Thus, they still had nearly $1.50 left for entertainment, savings, or whatever else they chose.[45]

Supporting a family on $5 or $6 or even $8 a week was of course, quite a different matter. Still worse off were those who supported brothers, sisters, children, or parents on as little as $2: Negro women, orphans who were too young to command adult wages, women who worked at home because they had to care for infants or invalids as well as support them. During the 1880's the New York *Tribune* told the stories of many such women. One was a widow of sixty-five who earned $2.70 a week by sewing. She lived and worked in a tenement room ten feet square, for which she paid 75 cents a week rent. She spent about 60 cents a week for food: 15 cents for a pound of wurst, 10 cents for a pound of cheese, 25 cents for five loaves of bread, 10 cents for tea, sugar and a penny's worth of milk on Sunday. The remaining half of her weekly wages she used to buy food for the family of a neighbor, a younger widow who was trying unsuccessfully to support two infants and an invalid father on wages of $5 a week.[16]

The attitudes of people toward their own conditions are always circumscribed by what they are accustomed to and what they can reasonably hope for. From today's vantage point, or even from the viewpoint of the middle and upper classes in 1890, the working women of 1890 labored under intolerable conditions. The average working woman, however, had no burning sense of being wronged. She went to work, not because she had to in order to eat, but because she thought that, on balance, she would be better off if she worked. What she got from work was usually very much what she had expected. If she had come from Europe, or from a poor farm in America, what she found was sometimes considerably better than what she had expected. When she thought of something still better, she was more likely to hope for an early marriage to a good husband than for an easier job or higher pay.

These simple truths exasperated the members of the special committee of the New York legislature which was inspired in 1895 by the influential Consumers' League to publicize working conditions in New York City factories and department stores. The committee had no trouble in exposing the cruel exploitation of women and children in the sweatshops of the garment and cigar industries. But it had little success in persuading retail clerks that they were mistreated. Indeed, investigators and witnesses looked at working conditions so differently that they often found it impossible to understand each other. The following interchange with a stock girl in Simpson and Crawford's dry goods store was typical:

Q. Suppose you had it in your power to make such changes as you wanted to . . . is there anything there that you would like to see changed or different from what it is now . . . ?
A. You might as well say, suppose I was Mr. Crawford.

Q. That is exactly it. . . . A. I don't know; I can't suggest anything to you; of course, if I was Mr. Crawford I would look after my own interests, wouldn't I? . . .

Q. You don't think you ought to get extra pay? A. That is a different question.

Q. No, that is not; I am afraid you are not frank with us. A. You are? . . .

Q. Let me ask you a question: you think you ought to get paid for overtime? A. Yes, sir.

Q. You would like to be able to ride up in the elevator to the lunch room or closets? A. Yes, sir. . . .

Q. And wouldn't you like, if you could, to have that closet further removed from the lunch room? A. I don't care how near it is . . . I don't eat up there. . . .

Q. Now, you have already told us three or four things that you would like to have changed; is there anything else that you think of? A. No, sir; I don't think of anything else. . . .

Q. What do you expect the first week when you are made a saleslady; how much of a raise? A. A dollar.

Q. After being in the firm five years, is that all you expect, $5 a week? A. That is all I can expect.

Q. I don't know what you ladies think about it, but I wish in my line of business that the employes would only anticipate receiving a dollar raise. . . . I can see . . . that you are a little afraid; there is no necessity for being afraid. *A.* I am not a bit afraid—not a bit. . . . The only thing I would like to see changed I would like later hours—get in later.

Q. About 9 o'clock would suit you? *A.* About 9 o'clock. . . .

Q. What time would you leave in the evening? *A.* I suppose I have got to say about 4 o'clock.

Q. No; we don't want to be too hard on the employer. *A.* Well I would like to go home about 5 o'clock.

About to give up, after failing to elicit complaints from another young woman, a legislator finally asked:

Q. And there is not anything that you are not satisfied with? *A.* Certainly not, or I wouldn't have stayed there as long as I have if I was not perfectly satisfied.

Q. How is it you have never received any increase in wages in all these years? *A.* I don't know, I never inquired. . . . I know it is my own fault; I went in late; and I have not interested myself I suppose. . . .

Q. Was your lateness due to the hard day's work previous to the day you came late? *A.* No. I was a little bit dilatory.

Q. You are never tired when you go home at night? *A.* No, sir.

Q. I wish I could say the same thing. *A.* We might as well make the best of our lot.[47]

Since department store employees worked under better conditions than most other women, it is not especially surprising to find them satisfied with their work. Cotton mill operatives in the South were not nearly so contented. In December, 1891, the North Carolina Commissioner of Labor Statistics sent out questionnaires to a group of textile mill workers, asking for information about their living and working conditions, and urging them to mention "any evils that may exist, the causes of their existence, and the proper remedies." Many of the respondents said that twelve hours a day was too long for women and children to work;

that they would be grateful for a ten-hour day. Others thought that the mills should not employ children, at least until they were twelve years old and had completed six grades in school. Some complained that they were paid in trade checks instead of cash, and that the checks were not redeemed at par. This system of fraud seemed to arouse more resentment than low wages, though some complained of low wages too.

On the other hand, few of the workers complained bitterly about working conditions that were much harder in many ways than in any other branch of American industry. Hours of work ranged from sixty-six to seventy-five. Wages were as low as 60 cents a week for children, and few of the girls and women made more than $3. Yet most of the respondents offered no suggestions for change, and most of those who did asked in mild terms for very modest improvements. A few volunteered that mill owners were not personally to blame, since they would not be able to compete if they improved conditions in their own mills. Some denounced the foolishness and extravagance of other workers, and placed the blame for child labor on greedy and short-sighted parents. Some pointed out that mill workers were much better off than they had ever been on the farms from which most of them came.

A young woman who earned forty cents a day thought that

the greatest need of the laboring class in this locality are facilities for intellectual development. We need zealous teachers who really desire to raise the masses to a higher plane of moral, intellectual and social attainments . . . and, when some degree of progress is attained in the above, we then need libraries, papers, and magazines. The greatest of the minor needs, I perceive, is an advancement in wages.

Wage increases were a minor need to this girl because her family was better off than most. Four of the six persons in the family worked in the mills. Together, they earned $620, and saved $180 during the year. But many of the other families also earned more than they spent. Although the average income of eighteen families which reported total family income and expenses was only $360, eleven of them reported that they spent less than they earned, by an amount which averaged nearly $100 per year.

A similar response came from two spinsters who had been working in a cotton mill since before the Civil War. They supported two relatives, probably aged parents. One of them wrote:

This is a country place, eleven miles to the nearest railroad station, consequently living is cheaper than around the towns. My sister and I earn 40 cents a day each, and we are able, by practicing close economy, to save something every month when we are paid in cash. We have a good, comfortable house, as much room as we need, rent free. The firm own a flour-mill and store, and there are both church and schoolhouse in the place, so, you see, we are well provided for. . . . Some of the families have a better chance than we do, but what I have said will apply pretty much to all hands here. . . . As you will see, I am an old hand. Thirty years of experience has taught me many things. I am certain that the condition of the working class of people would improve if they could be brought to understand the benefits of education, and parents would avail themselves of every opportunity for the education of their children.[48]

Like the department store workers of the North, the textile mill workers of the South were reasonably contented because life in the mills and the mill villages was a better life, for all its drawbacks, than most rural Southerners had ever known. Among the nation's millions of working

women there were, of course, many who were deeply discontented. Helen Campbell was able to fill column after
column in the New York *Tribune* with the bitter complaints of such women. She did this, however, by seeking
out women who had been reduced to circumstances far
inferior to those in their own past and to the conditions
of others around them. She wrote almost exclusively about
widows, orphans, and victims of epidemic, accident, desertion, fraud, theft, and rape.[49]

Most working women did not act as though they were
crushed by their lives as workers. North or South, they
had spirit and energy to fight on occasion, to sing and tell
ribald jokes over the noise of machines, to go home and
stay up half the night converting their last week's pay into
new dresses and hats for the following Sunday, to leave the
factory on Saturday night with a week's wages, and shop
until the last stores closed at midnight. At the end of her
first-hand account of the working women of New York
City, Dorothy Richardson admitted somewhat reluctantly
that "there is nobody so little concerned about herself and
her condition as the working woman herself. Taking everything into consideration, and in spite of conditions which
. . . seem irreconcilably harsh and bitter—in the face of all
this, one must characterize the working woman as a contented, if not a happy woman." [50] Conditions seemed "harsh
and bitter" to Miss Richardson, but not to most other factory women, because she had ambitions to return to the
genteel work and middle-class life she had left behind.
Eventually, she succeeded. After the laundry, she became,
successively, sales clerk, stenographer, secretary, and finally,
editor and writer.

There are still some economic backwaters in America where work is as hard and the rewards no greater than in 1890. But by and large, the danger, the cruelty, the threats to life and health, and even most of the sweat of work, have been removed. Whether the pace of work has slowed or not is a moot question, but there is no question that the combined impact of muscular effort, pace, noise, heat, dirt, danger, discomfort, and other stressful conditions has been greatly reduced. The remaining stresses of work, moreover, have become far lighter because the work week has been cut by one third, with additional time off for paid vacations, paid holidays, and paid sick leave. At the same time, of course, the rewards of work have increased many times. Today, the average annual income of families headed by semiskilled factory workers, truck drivers, and others whom the Census calls "operatives and kindred workers" is nearly $5,000.

In addition to more pay for less work, the American worker has also gained a good measure of security in his job and control over its terms. The employer's freedom to fine, fire, lay-off, reassign, promote, alter work loads, and otherwise change the employment relationship has been greatly curtailed. In a few situations characterized by large unions and small companies, employee control over the job has gone so far that no worker can be hired, fired, or even disciplined without the concurrence of the union. The economy has made considerable progress toward eliminating unemployment resulting from such causes as seasonal fluctuations in business, or changes in processes and products, and toward maintaining income when workers are laid off.

Perhaps the clearest indication of the extent to which the demands of work have been reduced and the rewards multiplied is the change in the flavor of controversy over the terms of work. Ever since the industrial revolution began in England more than two centuries ago, it has been accompanied by outraged protest against niggardly wages and the inhuman demands of work upon the bodies and spirits of men. Within the last two decades, however, this sense of moral indignation has virtually disappeared from the American scene, even from the rhetoric of organized labor.

To describe and explain how increasing productivity has been translated into easier work, better working conditions, higher pay, and greater security is beyond the scope of the present study. It would require detailed consideration of such developments as the growth of union power, changes in the relationship between government and the economy, management's growing awareness that its treatment of employees affects its profits, and the emergence of the principles and tools of personnel management.

Part of the reduction in the demands of work has been a by-product of technological development. Electric motors have replaced steam engines in American factories because they are cheaper and more flexible. But they are also quieter, cooler, cleaner, and safer. Similarly, manual tasks have been mechanized mainly to save time and money, or to turn out a better, more uniform product. But another result has been to eliminate jobs requiring heavy lifting, pushing, and carrying.

Mechanization is only one reason for the disappearance of much drudgery from American work. Another is the sharp decline in the number of workers directly involved in the production of goods, relative to the number engaged in design, control, management, sales, communication, record-keeping, and the provision of educational, recreational, medical, and other services. Between 1900 and 1950, according to one estimate, employment in service industries increased from less than 30 percent to more than half of total employment.[51] Moreover, even within the goods-producing industries, relatively fewer workers are directly engaged in production. Between 1947 and 1953, the number of nonproduction workers in manufacturing establishments increased by nearly one third, while the number of production workers remained nearly stationary.[52] Those developments have reduced the physical demands of work not only by minimizing manual labor, but also by eliminating the incidental physical strains associated with industrial processes. In spite of enormous progress toward making the factory a better place in which to work, the office is still safer, cleaner, and quieter.

Most of the jobs that do not involve direct production of goods require more education, training, and skill than is needed in most production jobs. Moreover, in spite of the fact that many traditional skilled occupations have nearly disappeared from the modern factory, factory work, too, requires more training for a higher proportion of workers than formerly. In short, technological progress and the expansion of service industries have both depended on improvement in the education and training of the American worker.[53]

All of these changes have affected both men and women workers, but in many ways the course of developments and their consequences have been different for women. Whether work is hard or easy, well- or ill-rewarded, almost

all men have to work, but most women do not. Consequently, the fact that employers have offered more pay
for constantly lighter work in more pleasant surroundings
has undoubtedly contributed to the steady increase in the
number of women willing to work. At the same time, however, the fact that large numbers of reasonably well-
educated women were willing to work, when the conditions
satisfied them, had a great deal to do with bringing about
changes in the character of work. Growth in the number
of white-collar jobs was in part a direct response to the
availability of qualified women to fill them. Moreover, the
desire of employers to attract more women into clerical
and secretarial work has certainly contributed to the disappearance of dirt and gloom from the typical office, to the
spread of the coffee-break, and to the short work week
and long vacations of white-collar workers. Indirectly, the
extension of such benefits to office workers has affected all,
for management cannot afford too great a disparity between working conditions in different parts of the same
company.

In teaching and nursing, too, the interaction between
supply and demand has led to vast improvements in the
conditions of work. In these fields the growth of demand
has been qualitative as well as quantitative. If the public
were still willing to provide most young people with no
more than six or eight years of schooling by teachers who
themselves had no better education, there would be no
teacher shortage, and the wages and working conditions
of teachers would be far below today's standards. When
the public began to demand high school graduation, normal
school training, and eventually college degrees for teachers,
there was no alternative but to raise salaries, grant tenure,

permit teachers more freedom, and improve classroom conditions.

The slow, steady increase in educational standards was sharply accelerated during the 1930's. Because it was so difficult to find jobs, young people stayed in school longer, and school districts had no difficulty in hiring college graduates, even without raising salaries or improving conditions. By the time prosperity returned, the new standards were widely accepted, but young college graduates were going into more attractive occupations, or into the armed forces. The problem of finding qualified teachers did not become acute during the 1940's because of the decline in the school-age population resulting from the low birth rates of the thirties. By the end of the decade, this respite was over. The schools and the public were faced with the fact that under conditions of high employment they could not maintain the educational standards they professed to accept without substantial improvements in the wages and working conditions of teachers.

Developments in nursing paralleled those in teaching. Until the 1930's almost all nursing service in hospitals was provided by students. Most graduate nurses were employed in taking care of well-to-do private patients. As the depression deepened, however, private patients became scarce. Hospitals permitted graduates to stay on, often at wages little better than they had earned as students. Between 1929 and 1937, the number of graduate nurses on general duty in hospitals increased from 4,000 to 28,000. The hospitals gained the benefit of better nursing services, which made it easier to take advantage of medical advances and to expand and alter the functions of hospitals. Training improved as students were relieved of many ward duties. And the graduates at least had food, a place to live, and a little money. By the end of the depression, doctors, patients, and hospital administrators had become dependent on the new system, and its medical advantages had proved too great to give up. In 1941, for the first time, the majority of graduate nurses, over 100,000, were employed in hospitals.[54] As in teaching, it soon became apparent that maintaining and further improving the standards of nursing care required a revolution in the traditional outlook on wages, hours, and working conditions.

By and large, women still earn much less than men. The median income of men employed at some time during 1956 was 2.7 times as high as the median for women. One reason is that far more women work only part time or part of the year. Among women in all occupations who work full time all year, median income is nearly two thirds that of men. Hourly wages of women factory workers average about 70 percent of men's wages, compared to perhaps 50 percent, or even less, in 1890.

Modest gains in the relative earnings of women are partly a result of their shifting occupational concentration—away from the lowest paid jobs in unskilled factory work, domestic service, and farm labor, and into somewhat better-paid white-collar and professional jobs. Women's gains also reflect the fact that today they usually receive the same pay as men when they do essentially the same work.

As a rule, however, men and women are still employed in different kinds of jobs, and wages and salaries in most women's jobs are lower than in most men's jobs. Teaching is one of the relatively few fields open alike to men and women. Although women public school teachers are now

paid the same as men with the same qualifications, teachers
as a group earn considerably less than workers in predominantly male occupations which require equivalent training.
And most of the better jobs in school administration go to
men.

In industry, women are more likely than men to work
for marginal businesses characterized by small size,
low capital investment, low profit margins, haphazard personnel practices, high employee turnover, and low pay.
Many thousands of women still work in such plants, making cheap clothing, costume jewelry, paper hats and party
favors, inexpensive toys, picture frames, knickknacks, and
similar products. Sometimes ignored by government and
union alike, these are the plants where conditions are most
likely to be reminiscent of the last century, even to the
crudely lettered "Operators Wanted" sign on the door.
Usually located in old buildings in run-down neighbor-
hoods, they draw upon the least educated and neediest
portion of the labor supply: Puerto Ricans, Negroes,
Mexicans, and poor white migrants from the rural South.
By comparison with 1890, fewer women are compelled by
need and lack of qualifications to take such jobs. Largely
because of the establishment of minimum standards, moreover, wages and working conditions in such businesses are
generally not so far below average as they were in 1890.
Nevertheless, women industrial workers still tend to be
concentrated in the industries and occupations which pay
the lowest wages.

As in 1890, most employers offer women little opportunity for training leading to promotion. Most large companies and many small ones today provide a great deal of
formal instruction for employees at all levels, but advanced

training programs are often restricted to men. Moreover, women are concentrated in fields of work where opportunities for promotion are limited, and where the opportunities which do exist offer not a great deal more pay than the ordinary employee receives. This is true of teaching, nursing, and most clerical and service jobs. In industry women are not often placed in jobs which normally constitute a step on the ladder of promotion to skilled or supervisory status. It is still true, in short, that most women end their working lives performing much the same tasks that they performed when they began work. Women rarely advance to jobs which pay high salaries for the exercise of great responsibility and specialized competence. Out of every 1,000 male employees, 153 earned $6,000 or more in 1956. But out of every 1,000 female employees, only nine reached the $6,000 level. Twenty-three men but only one woman in every 1,000 earned $10,000 or more.

Throughout the last six decades, efforts to improve the conditions of women's work have run in two currents. One current sprang from the argument that women are entitled to special consideration because of their primary function as mothers, and because they are weaker and more vulnerable than men. Since they seldom defended themselves through union action, it followed that they needed special legal protection. Supporters of protective legislation have usually stressed the plight of women who work because of necessity, and they have been concerned mainly with the lower ranks of female employees in factories, stores, restaurants, laundries, and similar establishments.

Between the turn of the century and World War I, state legislatures began to provide payments to widows and orphans so that mothers would not have to work. In many states women were barred from working nights, or more than a specified number of hours, or in certain arduous or dangerous occupations. Other laws regulated sanitation, ventilation, seating, and other physical circumstances of women's employment. Between 1912 and 1913, nine states passed minimum wage laws for women.

The significance of these developments extends far beyond their impact on women's work. Today, of course, a large body of protective labor legislation applies to men as well as women. The legal precedent for public regulation was first established, however, in the name of defenseless women and children. Almost all such legislation was first enacted and fought through the courts for their benefit, and much of it still applies only to them. The movement to protect women, moreover, was largely responsible for spreading information about working conditions and for arousing public revulsion against the despotism and inhumanity of some employers.

The second current of effort to improve the terms of women's work sprang from the desire to extend the educational and occupational opportunities of women and to eliminate policies, practices, and attitudes which make it difficult for women to compete on even terms with men. Since shortly after World War I, this viewpoint has been epitomized in the efforts of a coalition of professional women and businesswomen's organizations to abolish all legal recognition of differences between the sexes, including protective labor legislation which applies to women only. These groups have been strongly opposed by unionists, both male and female, by some religious groups, and by other women's organizations which insist on preserving special protection by law for women in general and women workers in particular.

Whatever the merits of this controversy, it serves to point up the fact that work means different things to different women. Today, as in 1890, the great majority of working women have little interest in achieving success in a career. In 1890 most of them were young girls who looked forward to a life in which paid work would have no part. Today, most of them are already married, and more concerned with their homes and families than their jobs.

In recent years employers have been able to attract millions of additional women into the labor force without changing the relative levels of men's and women's pay, or greatly expanding women's opportunities for advancement. The decade between 1945 and 1955 was one of booming prosperity, labor shortages, unprecedented peacetime demand for women workers, and unprecedented increase in the number of women working. Yet, in 1955, the median wage and salary income of women who worked full time was still less than two thirds that of men—almost exactly the same as it was in 1945. This suggests that it is not particularly important to a great many working women whether or not they earn as much as men, or have equal opportunities for training and promotion. What they seek first in work is an agreeable job that makes limited demands. Since they have little desire for a successful career in paid work, they are likely to drift into the traditional women's occupations. They are willing to become teachers, though they could earn more as engineers; willing to take factory and service and clerical jobs that hold little hope of substantial advancement.

From this point of view, paid work has improved

enormously since 1890. A wider variety of jobs are available. A whole new world of clean, respectable, sedentary clerical jobs has opened up for women. Almost all jobs are located in pleasanter surroundings, and require less time and less physical effort. Moreover, because wages and salaries have been rising steadily for almost two decades, a woman can now stay in the same job and still look forward to earning more and more.

On the other hand, there has long been a relatively small number of women who are moved by strong ambitions for wealth, success, or recognition through work. What they seek first in a job is the opportunity to compete for the larger prizes in business and the professions. For these women, too, the world of paid work has improved substantially. Women are admitted to almost all professional schools. Few people now believe, as most once did, that it is sinful for women to want a career, or that women are inherently incapable of high performance in a demanding job.

Yet the woman who urgently wants to develop and utilize her abilities in work still has barriers to overcome. Employers tend to judge all working women on the basis of their experience with the majority who are content with modest rewards for modest efforts. Many capable, ambitious women are held in jobs far below their capacity because women are not considered suitable candidates for training or promotion, and many others fail to develop their interests and abilities because they foresee only limited opportunities to use them in work.

Chapter IV

WOMEN, MEN, AND WORK: VALUES AND ATTITUDES

"THE LAW OF NATURE destines and qualifies the female sex for the bearing and nurture of the children of our race and for the custody of the homes of the world . . . in love and honor. And all life-long callings of women, inconsistent with these radical and sacred duties of their sex . . . are . . . when voluntary, treason against it," declared the Wisconsin Supreme Court in 1875. The Court conceded that "the cruel chances of life sometimes baffle both sexes, and may leave [some] women free from the peculiar duties of their sex. These may need employment, and should be welcome to any not derogatory to their sex and its proprieties, or inconsistent with the good order of society." The justices held, nevertheless, that "it is public policy to provide for the sex, not for its superfluous members; and not to tempt women from the proper duties of their sex by opening to them duties peculiar to ours"—not, in short, to grant the petition of a woman for admission to the bar of the Court.[1]

The fact that the Court was shortly overruled by the

legislature suggests that the judiciary had fallen behind the times. On the other hand, few Americans would have challenged the Court's initial premises, either in 1875 or for several decades thereafter. Nearly everyone believed that women's first duty was to bear and raise children and maintain the home, and that women were inherently better fitted for these than for any other functions. Likewise, nearly everyone agreed that it was sometimes necessary and proper for women to work, and that some jobs outside the home were suitable for some women.

There was wide disagreement, however, about the circumstances that justified a woman's going to work and about the particular jobs a woman might take. At one extreme, a great many Americans believed that no girl or woman should work unless compelled to by the absence of a male breadwinner, and that few jobs were appropriate for women. At the other extreme, a very small minority believed that every woman should be free to follow the career of her choice.

It is always difficult to measure attitudes, still more difficult to discover how attitudes influence behavior, and perhaps impossible to assess with any precision the role of changing attitudes in any series of historical events. The question of women's employment, however, involves two subjects which lie near the center of human emotions: work and the relationship between men and women. One may at least be certain, therefore, that changes in women's work have been profoundly influenced by what people have thought and felt about work and about women.

In the decades before and after the turn of the century, the employment of women was a major public issue. Like the judges of the Wisconsin Court, many Americans felt that it was akin to treason for a woman to want to work. Most of the arguments advanced to support this position were based on a common conception of the nature and role of women. In physique, temperament, and mentality, the argument ran, women are exquisitely specialized for their functions as mothers and guardians of the home. To employ a woman in any other way would endanger not only her essential female qualities but also her sanity, her health, and even her life. This view of woman implied a complementary view of man. As the home was woman's sphere, so the workplace was man's. Man was deficient in the feminine ideals of "tenderness, compassion . . . beauty and the harmonies of grace" essential to the creation of a true home; but abundantly endowed with the masculine qualities of "energy, desire, daring, and forcible possession" necessary in the world of business, government, and war.[2]

Even feminists sometimes admitted that women did not have all of the intellectual abilities of men. Mary Putnam Jacobi, physician and champion of women's rights, wrote in 1891 that "women cannot maintain the same intellectual standards as are established and maintained by men. The claim of ability to learn, to follow, to apply knowledge . . . does not imply a claim to be able to originate, or to maintain . . . the robust, massive intellectual enterprises which . . . are now carried on by masculine strength and energy."[3]

Another feminist pointed out that society seemed bent on turning men and women into distinct species, with hardly any characteristics in common.[4] The supposed inherent differences between the sexes were reenforced, in middle-class families, by education, upbringing, and dress. Once past the common school, girls turned to music, manners, sewing, and French, while mathematics, science, and the social sciences were left to boys. Girls were expected to play quietly, without running or shouting like their brothers. Even as small children they were often swathed in heavy dresses, and, if they followed fashion, their costume became more confining as they grew older. The nineties were the decade of the hourglass figure, constructed of wire bust-frame, tight-laced corset, bustle, and eight or nine petticoats.

This elaborate emphasis on sexual differences served to support the opposition to women's employment in several ways. In the first place, work was seen as a danger to both the health of women and their temperamental qualifications for motherhood. In any case, women lacked the physical, emotional, and mental qualifications for success in most jobs. Finally, if men and women were molded in such antithetical patterns, it seemed clear that the entire social order depended upon a precisely balanced adjustment of functions and relationships and that any disturbance of woman's position would topple the whole structure. In particular, the employment of women was viewed as a threat to moral standards, to the economic foundations of the family, and to the self-esteem of men.

The idea that the female body was an extremely delicate mechanism was an important element in the prevailing picture of women until near the end of the century. It was commonly believed that the female sexual organs were readily damaged by the pursuit of any unwomanly activity. The classic elaboration of this viewpoint was contained in two books by physicians published in the 1870's: *Sex in Education*, by Edward H. Clarke, and *Sex in Industry*, by Azel Ames. Clarke wrote:

Woman, in the interest of the race, is dowered with a set of organs peculiar to herself, whose complexity, delicacy, sympathies, and force are among the marvels of creation. If properly nurtured and cared for, they are a source of strength and power to her. If neglected and mismanaged, they retaliate on their possessor with weakness and disease, as well of the mind as of the body.

The central and most delicate feature of the female system, Clarke went on, is the menstrual function.

During the epoch of development, that is, from the age of fourteen to eighteen or twenty . . . the system . . . is peculiarly susceptible, and disturbances of the delicate mechanism we are considering, induced . . . by constrained positions, muscular effort, brain work, and all forms of mental and physical excitement, germinate a host of ills. Sometimes these causes, which pervade . . . our . . . schools . . . produce an excessive performance of the . . . function, and this is equivalent to a periodical hemorrhage. Sometimes they produce an insufficient performance of it; and this, by closing an avenue of elimination, poisons the blood, and depraves the organization. The host of ills thus induced are known to physicians . . . as amenorrhea, menorrhagia, dysmenorrhoea, hysteria, anemia, chorea, and the like.[5]

Ames accepted Clarke's version of female physiology without question. He devoted his own volume to demonstrating that industrial employment was at least as great a peril as education to proper menstruation, and hence to the health, sanity, and fertility of women. Both Clarke and Ames were eminent physicians whose opinions were cited with respect well into the present century. Clarke was

Professor of Materia Medica at Harvard for seventeen years. The Ames volume was an expansion of a report prepared for and published by the Massachusetts Bureau of Labor Statistics, whose commissioner, Carroll D. Wright, later became the first United States Commissioner of Labor.[6]

That these viewpoints were taken seriously is indicated by the action of the Associated Collegiate Alumnae in 1882. One of the first tasks undertaken by the newly formed organization was a study to determine whether college education had, in fact, damaged the health of women. A list of questions was drawn up with the help of a panel of physicians and sent to all 1,290 women college graduates in the United States. The responses were turned over to the Massachusetts Bureau of Labor Statistics. The Bureau reported that 77.87 percent of the respondents were in good health, while only 17.02 percent were in poor health—which seemed to give college women a good margin of healthiness over other women.[7]

By the end of the century it was generally acknowledged that women were much sturdier than Ames and Clarke had imagined—sturdy enough to stand the physical strains of higher education and of many jobs. Most people still believed that women were much weaker and more vulnerable than men, but this belief was usually cited as a reason for regulating their working conditions, rather than for not educating or employing them.

Even before the extreme views of women's physical weakness were discredited, arguments against their employment were usually based on psychological rather than physiological grounds. In either case, the approach was much the same. Nearly everyone agreed that women were born with certain mental and emotional traits which were indispensable to the performance of their duties and the well-being of society. On the other hand, it was commonly believed that even the connubial and maternal instincts were exceedingly vulnerable. Thus, Grant Allen, a well known scientific popularizer, wrote in *The Forum* for June 1889:

All that is distinctly human is man—the field, the ship, the mine, the workshop; all that is truly woman is merely reproductive—the home, the nursery, the schoolroom. There are women, to be sure, who inherit much of male faculty, and some of these prefer to follow male avocations; but in so doing they for the most part unsex themselves; they fail to perform satisfactorily their maternal functions.[8]

Industrial employment was dangerous, from this viewpoint, because it threatened "to eliminate the truly feminine girl . . . and to produce a heavy, rough type comparable to the peasant women of Europe." [9] But professions such as medicine, law, and journalism were equally perilous. Wrote the Wisconsin judge whose opinion has already been cited:

It would be . . . shocking to man's reverence for womanhood and faith in woman, on which hinge all the better affections and humanities of life, that women should be permitted to mix professionally in all the nastiness of the world which finds its way into courts of justice; all the unclean issues, all the collateral questions of sodomy, incest, rape, seduction, fornication, adultery, pregnancy, bastardy, legitimacy, prostitution, lascivious cohabitation, abortion, infanticide, obscene publications, libel and slander of sex, impotence, divorce.[10]

A milder statement of the conflict between femininity and the requirements of work appeared after the turn of the century in an occupational compendium called *Workers of the Nation*. The author, Gilson Willets, warned the young woman with journalistic aspirations that she would have to accustom herself to a "shirt-sleeve environment and a tobacco-laden atmosphere," learn not to cough "when the smoke from a cigarette happens to float her way," and never admit that she may have a headache. Moreover, "she is obliged to approach men to whom she has never been introduced, and talk to them," and to "interview murderers and make analytical studies of criminals of the most degraded kind." [11]

Warnings such as these were often contrasted with the ennobling spectacle of the pure and tender mother, carefully nurtured from childhood to fulfill her position in the center of her brood of happy children. On a somewhat more selfish plane, one author wrote in 1894 that woman should never work because men "wish her to be beautiful, attractive, and full of grace." He declared that outward beauty was but the sign of inner serenity, and that "the emotions which toil entails . . . are violent and strong emotions . . . which cannot endow her with the attractiveness of grace." [12]

Purity, modesty, and lack of passion were among the most valued of the qualities generally attributed to women. Since men were viewed as naturally lustful and aggressive, women's reticence seemed to serve as the principal defense of moral standards. Like other essential feminine qualities, however, the virtuous instincts were viewed as extremely vulnerable. To prevent their defeat, it was necessary to minimize young women's opportunities for unsupervised association with men, and to isolate them from any source of knowledge about or interest in sex. Indeed, polite convention insisted that there be no reference in public to the physical basis of sex. Ladies were expected to refer, if absolutely necessary, to limbs rather than legs. There were even some—in the seventies and eighties if not later—who clothed the limbs of their pianos in modest ruffles. The girl who did not live up to such ideals of feminine propriety was likely to be viewed as a temptress and an outcast. Thus, in 1886 a police court judge in Toledo, Ohio, was reported to have discharged a prisoner who had been arrested for "insulting" a woman, on the ground that "no honest woman has occasion to be out alone on the streets . . . after half-past ten o'clock at night." [13]

Going to work was often viewed in the same light as being out alone after ten-thirty. Employment, it was felt, brought women into close association with men under particularly demoralizing circumstances. Dr. Ames dealt at length with the moral as well as the physiological dangers of work.

The influences that bring about . . . moral . . . perversions are notably abundant in . . . industrial employments. The disregard paid the decencies of life in the location and condition of water-closets, etc.; the laxity with which clothing is worn, and postures are assumed, in the processes of manufacture; the constant association of both sexes . . . the temperature, excitement of emulation, etc., are all actively operative for evil. . . .[14]

The belief that women's employment was likely to lead to immorality was expressed as late as 1908 by no less an authority than the Supreme Court of the United States in the well-known case of *Muller v. Oregon*. In upholding an Oregon statute limiting the hours of women's work, the court sustained the argument of Louis D. Brandeis, counsel for the state. The Brandeis brief declared, with abundant citations from European and American authorities, that the prevailing ten-hour workday was likely to leave a woman exhausted, her higher instincts dulled, craving only excitement and sensual pleasure.

Many Americans saw the employment of women as a threat to men and their role in society as well as to women. Every depression brought a resurgence of the complaint that working women were stealing jobs that belonged to men. In 1894, as the economy sank deeper into the most serious depression in the nation's history, one critic declared that "woman-labor . . . only tends to lower the marketable value of male labor; for while woman is working in the factories, there are everywhere . . . crowds of men vainly seeking employment . . ." [15] In the same year, Congress called upon the Bureau of Labor to investigate the employment of women, "and the effect, if any . . . upon the wages and employment of men." The Bureau collected data showing that the employment of women had been increasing faster than the employment of men for several decades, and reported itself certain that "females are to some extent entering into places at the expense of . . . males." [16]

Women who worked even though they did not "need to" were a special target. The single woman who lived at home, whose father and brothers were employed, and who worked only for "pin money" was viewed as a prime menace, not only to breadwinning men but also to other women who had to work. Mrs. John Van Vorst ended her study of women's working conditions with the observation that this was the only real problem she had encountered. "In the masculine category," she wrote, "I met but one class of competitor: the bread-winner. In the feminine category I found a variety of classes: the bread-winner, the semi-bread-winner . . . the girl who is supported and spends all her money on her clothes." This, she found, "inevitably drags the wage level." Her suggested remedy was to eliminate these women from the competitive arena by opening schools where they could learn artistic handcrafts they could pursue at home.[17]

The female breadwinner probably did suffer from the competition of the girl who worked for pin money. On the other hand, several careful studies of men's and women's jobs showed that women were rarely hired for the same jobs as men, and therefore were not often in direct competition with them.[18] It is true that women sometimes replaced men when the nature of the work was drastically altered so as to create new and different jobs. But the reverse was also true. Throughout the second half of the century, changes in the structure and technology of the garment and textile industries—the two industries employing the most women—were accompanied by a steady increase in the ratio of men to women workers.

This was no consolation, however, to men who saw the demand for their skills reduced by the introduction of machines operated by women. Shortly after the turn of the century, for instance, women were being hired to operate cigar-making machines at one third the wages of skilled men who made cigars by hand. The latter were not likely to remember that the jobs of skilled women cigar makers were also threatened, nor to recognize that mechanization was inevitable, whether or not women were hired to operate the new machines. To the male members of the cigar makers unions, machines, cheap cigars, the tobacco trust, and women workers were all part of the same evil.

To many observers the textile industry provided an even clearer example of the pernicious effects of women's employment. The majority of mill employees were women or children. Wages for adult men were lower than in any other major industry. Moreover, the jobs held by most of the men were not much different from the jobs held by women and children. To some critics, therefore, it appeared that the wages of men were held down by the competition of women and children. Generally, however, the blame was not placed on the women and children who worked, but on millowners who attracted families by offering jobs to women and children rather than by paying a living wage to men, or on men who were willing to work for so little that their wives and children had to take jobs.

The textile towns were inhabited largely by families who welcomed the abundant employment opportunities for women and children. Within the more prosperous segments of the population, however, men were expected to support their families without help. When a man permitted female relatives to work, several damaging inferences were possible: that he could not support them; that he refused to protect them from the multiple dangers of the world of work; or that he had no control over what they did. One young woman who went to work during the depression of the nineties pointed out that she was the only woman wage earner in a very large family. Twenty years later she wrote that she could

hear some of the spurious wails yet. One good relative . . . warned me it would totally ruin my manners for society. Another good dame . . . used to sit bewailing by the hour that her "dear girls should ever need to work." She had set her face like flint against that need, telling her daughters that it was the duty of "father and brothers to take the blasts of the world," till the father took so many blasts that he ran away to New York. . . .[19]

Mary Austin did not learn until after she married that her husband had substantial debts. In the California town where they lived in the late nineties, the fact that he had made no effort to pay was not regarded as a serious fault. Much more damaging to his prestige, she found, was her own attempt to help him repay his creditors by taking a job as a teacher. One of his close friends took her aside, she later wrote, "to impress upon me the extraordinary liberality of my husband's mind in allowing me to earn money." [20]

In middle-class circles the employment of wives or daughters was taken as a sign of masculine failure. Conversely, one of the most acceptable ways for a man to display his success and bolster his prestige was to keep his wife and daughters in luxurious idleness. In 1884 a socialist journal commented on this tendency with a parody of the wedding service which began with the following lines:

> O wilt thou take this form so spare,
> This powdered face and frizzled hair—
>   To be thy wedded wife;
> And keep her free from labor vile,
> Lest she her dainty fingers soil—
>   As long as thou hast life? [21]

Oddly enough, however, another part of the case against women's employment was based on misgivings over extravagant expenditures on and by women. A common complaint about the working girl was that she wasted her wages on elaborate dress. A variant on this theme held that the contrast between her own poor lot and the pampered condition of her betters was likely to engender a compelling desire for luxuries she could not afford. The department store girl who spent her days selling silks and satins to the idle rich was especially vulnerable, according to the folklore of the time. In either case, whether she grew accustomed to luxury or wanted luxury she could not afford, the conclusion was the same. The ex-working girl was accused of bringing to marriage a heritage of reckless ambition which often drove her husband to ceaseless toil, debt, ruin, and an early death.

Dreiser's *Sister Carrie* illustrates this as well as many other facets of the case against women's work. On the train to Chicago, Carrie's young and innocent beauty has the inevitable effect on Charles Drouet, traveling salesman, a "nice, good-hearted man," but also a practiced "masher." Drouet then passes out of the picture long enough for the city to beat her into a state of receptiveness to his advances. Broken in health and spirit by drudgery, low pay, and lack of a winter coat, envious of the warm, elegant clothing she sees on the streets and in the store windows, Carrie meets Drouet again. The protecting constraints of family life have been replaced by the anonymity and moral indifference of the city. Her conscience puts up a losing fight, and she is soon installed in modest luxury as the salesman's mistress.

Carrie soon succumbs, however, to the lure of still greater luxury in the person of Hurstwood, prosperous manager of a fashionable saloon. Hurstwood intends only a harmless dalliance, but he is drawn by Carrie's charm, and driven by a spendthrift wife to run away with Carrie and his employer's money. Removed to New York, Hurstwood continues to play the role of the successful, protective male, spending incautiously, and concealing from Carrie all news of his diminishing fortunes. Even when he is unemployed, demoralized, and nearly penniless, he protests Carrie's suggestion that she go to work. Still drawn by glamor and luxury, however, she finds a job in the theater where her quick success contributes to Hurstwood's complete moral decay. At the end of the novel, Hurstwood has killed himself and Carrie is a star, famous, wealthy, alone, and deeply discontented. Carrie is a woman out of her element, destroying herself and others in her bewildered efforts to fit into an alien world. This, Dreiser says in effect, is what must happen when a girl is drawn by dreams and ambitions to the city and its work: unless, of course, she becomes enmeshed in a still darker catastrophe such as the seduction, betrayal, and murder of the working-girl heroine of *An American Tragedy*.

The 1890 stereotype of the woman who remained in her element showed her as a delicate vine clinging for support to man, the sturdy oak. As dutiful wife and mother, she created in the home a sanctuary for all the higher virtues. It is true that this stereotype was fading by the last decade of the century. The extent of its continuing power is suggested, however, by a paper read in 1887 to the emancipated members of the Association for the Advancement of Women. "Home Studies for Women," by Rebecca N. Hazard, suggested the proper course for a woman who longed to broaden her horizons and enrich her experience. The author began with a condescending look backward to "the time when it was not thought becoming for women to be over wise." She recalled "Mrs. Lincoln's Botany," specially written for girls, with no reference to the "distinction of sex in plants." She remembered, too, Washington Irving's sketch of the perfect wife: "To live in a cottage! Wear white gowns and a rose in the hair! To have strawberries and cream for tea, and to go forth with a smile each

evening to meet the returning 'Leslies' fresh from their
struggles with the world. . . ."

"We live in a different world now," she continued, a
world in which "the treasures of knowledge are no longer
withheld from women." Yet, there was still a problem. Man
applied and strengthened his knowledge in "the jostle and
excitement of the bread-winner's life," but as for women,
"no matter where she may stray . . . through stress of
circumstances, the home is her dream of Paradise. . . .
How then shall this inner shrine of the temple be made to
serve not only the ethical and moral purposes to which it
is allied, but how shall it be made to strengthen and stimu-
late thought?"

The answer was the home study club, where women
could "develop the thinking faculties and quicken the as-
sent [sic] from the realm of nature into that of spirit" by
reading to each other, studying, and discussing the "great
world-poets, Homer, Dante, Shakespeare, and Goethe." Of
all the poets, she went on, "Dante . . . should hold the
first place. . . . The young girl as well as the mature
matron can study the unsullied page of this poet without
misgiving. . . . No expurgated editions necessary! No
emotions awakened but those of profound reverence . . ."

The proper study of Dante required "a cheerful, sunny
room" in which "will be gathered five or six matrons, with
as many enthusiastic young girls. . . . Needle-work and
knitting will be found valuable assistants in putting all at
ease and preparing them for conversation. The most timid
girl will venture to talk . . . if fortified by some homelike
employment. . . ." Encouraged by visions of sunny rooms
and home study clubs across the land, the author concluded

that "we may . . . look with confidence to a nobler womanhood which will brighten and bless the future." [22]

Smile as we may at Mrs. Hazard's notion of progress, the distance from merely knitting to knitting with Dante did, in fact, represent progress against the effort to confine women strictly to maternal and wifely duties. Her own activities were not confined to these functions, nor even to home study. Mother of five children, she was also one of the early leaders of the woman suffrage movement, a founder of the Association for the Advancement of Women, and a lifelong crusader for the protection of Negroes, orphans, and working girls.[23]

Most women with such interests held very different views of women's nature and functions. The active proponents of women's rights are generally grouped together under the heading of feminists. Never very numerous, most of them were professional women—doctors, lawyers, writers, or women who made careers out of reform. To the contention that women were destined by nature for the home they responded with an explicit appeal to democratic principles: the essential equality of all human beings, the dignity of the individual, the right to self-determination.

In practice, the feminist demand for democratic treatment was a claim for recognition of the basic equality of men and women. In the economic sphere this meant that women should have the same freedom as men to choose and prepare for a career consistent with their interests and abilities. Instead of being stigmatized because they worked for pay, feminists wanted tolerance, respectability, even encouragement.

They invariably agreed that maternity was woman's highest function. They refused, however, to draw the conclusion that every woman should spend her whole life in the home. One of the pioneer women physicians conceded, in 1890, that

it is easy to feel that all the . . . worth and significance of women are summed up in the exquisite moments of . . . [motherhood]; easy to dread the introduction of other interests lest the women be unduly diverted from this, which is supreme. Yet nothing is more obvious than that . . . these moments are preceded by many years, and followed by many years, and for many women, through no fault of their own, never come at all. The seventy years of a lifetime will contain much waste, if adjusted exclusively to the five or six years of even its highest happiness.[24]

A woman lawyer refused to believe that

all women, or any woman, should stay inside of four walls continually to cook, wash dishes, sweep, dust, make beds, wash, iron, sew, etc. Oh, no! A woman may properly act as the custodian of a home and maintain it in love and honor, and do none of these things. . . . To stifle the longings of an immortal soul to follow any useful calling in this life [is] a departure from the order of nature.[25]

Similarly, the feminists did not doubt that women were specially equipped for their maternal functions, but they also believed that women's distinctive nature was robust enough to withstand considerable stress. Thus, while accepting the general proposition that men are stronger than women, they ridiculed the notion that the female organism was too delicate to tolerate any physical or mental strain beyond the range of maternity and housework. They argued that the relative weakness of women was mainly the result of ignorance, foolish dress, bad diet, and lack of

exercise, and set out energetically promoting health education, dress reform, sound diets, calisthenics, and women's
sports. They were delighted by displays of female physical
prowess, such as the heavy steel chain forged by a woman
blacksmith which was shown at the New Orlean's Exposi-
tion of 1885.[26] As far as the physical dangers of work were
concerned, feminists often pointed out that anyone who
could stand childbirth had nothing to fear from most jobs.
They argued, moreover, that the physical and mental activity involved in working were likely to improve rather
than impair a woman's ability to bear and raise healthy children.

While the feminists sought to minimize the differences
in physical strength and stamina between men and women,
they were often willing to admit the existence of important mental and temperamental differences. In response to
a query from the national headquarters of the Association
for the Advancement of Women, officers of the state chapters reported, in 1888, that women were inferior to men in
"power of original thought," in "matters of finance or business ability," in "all industrial enterprises requiring large
outlay of capital without certainty of return," in "those
vocations requiring a life-long devotion to an idea, or such
as to allow no deviation from fixed methods," and in matters "where large foresight involving great judgment is
concerned." They also believed that women were superior
to men in "delicacy of perception and manipulation," in
"their remarkable power of devotion," in "artistic needle-
work and decorative art," in "all that relates to patient,
routine work" and "attention to details," and in their
greater "fidelity, industry, integrity, purity, and sobriety." [27]

Feminists, of course, were not in full agreement among

themselves on woman's essential character. While some were willing to concede that women were inherently unsuited for certain tasks, others were inclined to minimize all differences between men and women or to see only the ways in which women were superior. They all agreed, however, that most of the mental and emotional inadequacies displayed by women in paid employment were the result of false education, not of innate qualities. On the contrary, they argued, it was just because of these special qualities that properly trained women were eminently suited for a variety of positions in the world of work, such as teacher, nurse, typist, bookkeeper, sales clerk, or editor of the woman's page of a newspaper. This was a powerful argument, for it was difficult to deny that a woman was more appropriately employed than a man in the tasks of selling yard goods, teaching the primary grades, or writing about recipes and fashions. It was even more difficult to counter the argument that the delicacy of a female client demanded the services of a female doctor or lawyer.

The feminists turned the stereotype of unique feminine qualities to their own purpose in still another way. They contended that the large affairs of government and business had been too long dominated by the crude, warlike, acquisitive, hardheaded, amoral qualities of men. Far from fearing that femininity would be endangered by contact with man's world, they argued that government and industry should no longer be deprived of the tempering influence of women's compassion, spirituality, and moral sensitivity. As Julia Ward Howe declared, "the very intensity of our feeling for home, husband, and children gives us a power of loving and working outside of our homes, to redeem the world as love and work only can." [28] Thus, the feminists did not always see themselves doing the same things in the same ways as men. Many of them felt, rather, that women were especially suited to fill a particular range of jobs, and that they could bring to other jobs their own special brand of superior qualifications.

The decades between 1880 and World War I were the age of "the new woman." Women were fighting for much more than the right to work in occupations of their choice. They insisted upon admission to colleges, universities, and professional schools. They argued in the courts and lobbies of the legislatures to expand the narrow rights of married women and widows under the common law. They rallied behind the temperance crusade and the suffrage movement. And they withstood ridicule and worse in defense of their freedom to join clubs, speak in public, ride bicycles, and engage in a host of other activities.

Opposing views of women's employment were only one part of a much broader controversy over women's place in life. As women gained increasing freedom, the champions of women's rights were encouraged to demand still greater and faster changes. On the other hand, the prospect of further change in so basic an aspect of human life inevitably led to widespread uneasiness and a determined defense of the status quo.

Traditional forms of family life and accepted patterns of relationships between the sexes were profoundly affected by the rapid expansion of the urban, industrial economy during the last quarter of the nineteenth century. Urban work and urban life took some members of the family away from home to factories, offices, shops, and schools for the greater part of each day. They became less dependent on each other, not only for food and shelter, but also for educational, medical, religious, police, and other services. Increasingly self-sufficient city residents tended to go their own ways. The traditional large family, with several generations of relatives under one roof, gradually broke up into smaller units, which usually included no more than husband, wife, and minor children. The divorce rate doubled between 1880 and 1900. In the absence of data on desertion and remarriage, it was not clear what this meant, but it was often taken as proof that more and more families were being completely dissolved. At the same time, the number of children per family was shrinking steadily. The public prints were filled with debates over the trend toward "race suicide," a trend which seemed especially ominous since everyone agreed that the best people were having the fewest children.

To many Americans, these developments seemed to portend the rapid disintegration of the family and its moral influence. In every large city thousands of young people lived alone, outside the reach of parental discipline. Even those who lived with their families were found to be less amenable to authority, at least in part because they were supporting themselves, or knew that they could. Moreover, in the city young people were constantly tempted by such demoralizing influences as the theater, the saloon, and the dance hall. Indeed, many thought that the city was little better than Satan's outpost. In 1911 the report of the Chicago Vice Commission expressed the suspicion that the decay of the family, the employment of women, the entrance of women into politics, and prostitution were all reflections of the impact of modern urban life on "the tastes, the possibilities, [and] the opportunities" of women in general. The report implied that the respectable women of Chicago were in a good position to understand the prostitute, because both had been infected by such features of modern life as "love of ease and luxury," the "craving for excitement and change," "lack of both ethical teaching and religious conviction," and "the economic stress of industrial life . . . with its enfeebling influence on the will power." This was all rather vague, but the Commission left no doubt about its meaning when it declared that "the whole tendency of modern life, which places a greater strain on the nervous system of both men and women of all classes than has even been placed . . . in the history of the civilized world, cannot but help . . . develop considerable eroticism." [29]

Another disturbing development was the growing distance between the activities and aspirations of women and old ideals of feminine functions. The capable homemaker was, of course, one of the oldest and most cherished ideals of womanhood. Women gained status and satisfaction by being first out with the wash on Monday morning, by baking the best pies, producing the best butter, collecting the most eggs, doing the fanciest needlework, stretching their husband's income as far as inconspicuous economy could make it go, and performing a host of other traditional tasks. The advance of the urban, industrial economy, however, had already eliminated many of these activities from the middle-class housewife's repertoire, and left some women wondering just what they ought to be doing.

There was also another and perhaps equally important effect. In an increasingly pecuniary society there was a tendency to make money the measure of all value, including the value of work. But most of women's household work received no monetary reward. Since urban husbands worked away from home, women could not even feel, as they could on a farm, that they were an integral part of a money-making team. Some believed that their work at home would never be fully appreciated unless it was appropriately rewarded with money, and there was a rash of proposals around the turn of the century to put the housewife on a salary. Another series of proposals aimed at elevating the prestige of housework by improving the training and pay of servants and trying to attract a higher type of girl into service. This was also the time when home economics emerged as a specialized field of study with the goal of professionalizing "home making." [30]

Even more troublesome was the fact that women were doing, or seemed anxious to do, many of the same things that men did. To a great many men the feminist demand for equal rights was an attempt to usurp masculine functions and prerogatives which could succeed only by forcing the traditional feminine role on men. One male reaction to the new woman is suggested by newspaper and magazine cartoons showing complete reversal of masculine and feminine behavior. One box would depict a group of big, square-jawed, black-suited women smoking cigars, drinking in saloons, discussing business, or making speeches to elect a woman as President. A second box would show a frail, aproned little man washing dishes, sweeping floors, or feeding the baby. [31]

From this point of view the very foundations of American society were rapidly crumbling under the impact of urbanization, industrialization, and the expanding privileges of women. The opposition to women's employment was concerned with far more than their place in the world of work. It was an integral part of a comprehensive effort to bring women back into the shelter of the home, to reemphasize their functions in the family, to reconstruct the supposedly tottering family around them, to reassert the authority of a strict moral code, and to restore a clear boundary between masculine and feminine character and behavior.

This was one extreme in the spectrum of attitudes toward woman's changing place in life and work. The feminists occupied the other extreme. They saw in the past history of the family a dismal record of man's enslavement of woman, at first through superior strength, later through control over custom, law, and the purse. Conversely, the loosening of family ties, the growing independence of the members of the urban family, the rise in the divorce rate, and the decline in the birth rate were all viewed not as signs of decay, but as the first, inadequate steps toward women's emancipation.

The feminists deplored the values which required a woman to stay married to a brutal, drunken, irresponsible, or merely indifferent husband, to submit to his desires, bear his children, and struggle to bring them up decently. One woman who renounced marriage for a career remembered her first childhood awareness of her mother's sadness.

What I wanted to ask was the question— Is it the common lot of woman to suffer in mute heartbreak? . . . Does it do any good, this suffering? What's it for? Why? I have been seeking the answers to those questions all my life. . . . The woman with the feckless husband, the mother with the spendthrift son, the sister with the no-good brother, the girl with the just-one-more chance lover all have to answer that question.[32]

In the opinion of some feminists even the best of marriages involved women in the "ever recurrent expectation of maternity and the demanding, unremitting care of children. . . . That sexual desire was something to which God . . . had sacrificed all women was so much a shibboleth of the period that it was not even successfully camouflaged by teachers and preachers with blague about the sacredness of motherhood." This, Mary Austin knew, was what her mother had in mind when she agreed to send her daughter to college "on the solemn promise that . . . she wouldn't 'throw it all away on some man.' " [33] The opportunity to work for pay seemed to offer an escape from dependence on men. If a woman could support herself in honor, she could refuse to marry or stay married, except on her own terms. Thus, work was seen by many feminists as an actual or potential alternative to marriage, and consequently, as an instrument for reforming the marriage relationship.

The feminists agreed with their most conservative opponents that the conditions of urban work and life were likely to make young girls susceptible to immoral advances. But they offered a simple economic interpretation of the cause and cure for immorality: girls went wrong because they were dependent on and oppressed by men, because they did not have the knowledge or opportunity to support themselves adequately. Education and a decent job, therefore, would protect them from the temptations of sin.

The feminists had no regrets about upsetting old ideals of masculine and feminine roles. Their major complaint was that change had not gone far enough. Thus, Charlotte Gilman wrote, in 1903, that

the home has not developed in proportion to our other institutions, and by its rudimentary condition it arrests development in other lines. . . . The two main errors in the right adjustment of the home to our present life are these: the maintenance of primitive industries in a modern industrial community, and the confinement of women to those industries and their limited area of expression.

In order to free women from more of their household tasks, she urged an elaborate communal organization, with groups of families living together and sharing the services of a staff of professional cooks, housekeepers, and children's nurses.[34]

The aim of the feminist attack on housework was to free women for the pursuit of more valuable and satisfying activities: self-improvement, community service, or work. Convinced that women had essentially the same needs as men, they saw in work not just a chance to earn money and become independent, but a way of gaining success, prestige, and a sense of personal fulfillment. They had only ridicule for the idea that women were usurping men's jobs, aping men's activities, threatening male status. Indeed, their support of the right to work was only one plank in a platform calling for the total overthrow of the male as defender and sole support of women, and ruler of the family, the economy, and the state. They continued to find inspiration in the "Declaration of Sentiments," a "Statement of Grievances to King Man" drawn up at the first Woman's Rights Convention at Seneca Falls, New York, in 1848. Patterned on the Declaration of Independence, the manifesto declared that "the history of mankind is a history of repeated injuries and usurpations on the part of man toward woman, having in direct object the establishment of an absolute tyranny over her." [35] Sixty-six years later, another woman put similar thoughts into less elegant form when she wrote

that the man who called himself "woman's natural
tector" was likely to "break her protected head." [36]

The two extreme views of women's place in life were
both confined largely to the middle and upper classes, and,
in many respects, both were very much at odds with the
experience and common-sense conclusions of most people.
A family had to have the means to support its women in
sheltered idleness before it could come to believe that this
was their natural state. The less sheltered and leisurely a
girl's life at home, the smaller was the contrast between life
at home and life at work, and the less reason to be disturbed
if she took a job. The distance was far greater from the
sewing room to the office than from the farm or tenement
to the factory. Even among the middle and upper classes
many found it difficult to swallow the whole argument for
keeping women at home. The constant influx of migrants
and immigrants and their steady climb up the urban social
hierarchy impeded the development of a strong tradition of
gentility. Many successful Americans were still too close
to working-class or impoverished agricultural origins to
have forgotten how their mothers and sisters worked.

Those who found it convenient to employ women had
their own picture of women's special qualities. Hundreds
of employers were questioned in 1895 by the U.S. Bureau
of Labor about their reasons for employing women in pref-
erence to men. The most common response was that
women were more adaptable to the particular work assigned to them. Other frequent answers were that women
"are more reliable, more easily controlled, cheaper, more
temperate, more easily procured, neater, more rapid, more

industrious, more careful, more polite, less liable to strike, learn more rapidly, etc." [37] On the other hand, when employers were asked why they did not promote women or pay them higher wages, they usually responded with the conventional picture of women's limitations.

The ideology of women's dependence was essentially an Eastern as well as a middle- and upper-class phenomenon. On the Great Plains and in the Far West, women continued to demonstrate their capacity to do nearly everything that men did, and raise children besides. The thousands of women who preempted or homesteaded land on their own account were probably the largest group of independent career women in the country. The shortage of women throughout the West led men to treat them with deference and even reverence. In the East deference toward women was likely to be reserved for those who followed genteel convention. But a lone woman could be reasonably sure of receiving polite treatment in the wildest parts of the West. Women had more legal rights in the West than in most Eastern states, and by 1900 four Western states had given them the vote.

The argument against women's employment ran into conflict not only with the facts of life as most people knew them, but also with the traditional American respect for work. Unlike Europe, where the top of the social structure was still occupied by the idle rich, America had never tolerated a leisured class, and it was not really prepared to tolerate a leisured sex. Nor was approval of work for women confined to household tasks. As the factory spread from New England to other regions, one of the commonest arguments in its favor was that it gave women a chance to perform more useful work. In the first years of the republic

Washington agreed with Hamilton's conclusion that the development of industry would make possible "the employment of persons who would otherwise be idle," and that "women and children are rendered more useful . . . by manufacturing establishments, than they would otherwise be." [38]

During the first decades of the nineteenth century the factory was often celebrated as the salvation of women who would otherwise be "doomed to idleness and its inseparable attendants, vice and guilt," and as an encouragement to early marriage and large families. [39] Much later in the century, the same comments greeted the industrialization of the South. In 1891, for instance, a printer in rural North Carolina complained that "there are no factories in this locality that employ unskilled labor over three or four months in the year, hence the women and children are left in a bad way for want of employment." [40] Historically, therefore, the employment of girls and women outside the home was greeted with approval as well as with misgivings. It was always assumed, however, that most women would be fully occupied at home. The special advantage of industry was that it turned to good use the time and energy of spinsters and young boys and girls who were not fully occupied in household or agricultural tasks.

Like their most determined opponents, the feminists also came into conflict with both the facts of life and the values of most Americans. In casting themselves as champions of freedom, they grossly exaggerated the extent to which women were oppressed by men. When they discussed women's legal status, for instance, they invariably cited Blackstone. Now it is true that Blackstone's interpretation of the common law gave very few rights to married women, and that Blackstone was enormously influential in the courts of most of the states. But it is also true that the principles of equity had always shielded women from men who sought to abuse their common-law rights.[41] In any case, by the end of the century the more severe legal disabilities of married women had been removed by statute.

Similarly, in the economic sphere, it is true that women were heavily dependent on men, in the sense that men still provided and controlled most of the money income of families. But it is also true that men relied heavily on the work of women, not only for raising their children and keeping their houses in order, but for a good deal of the necessities of life as well. Moreover, women were never as lacking in opportunities to earn a living as the feminists pretended. For generations, single, widowed, and deserted women had been supporting themselves as seamstresses, farmers, factory workers, proprietors of lodging houses, even occasionally as owners of small businesses. Earlier in the century it had been impossible for women to obtain professional training or to get white-collar jobs. But well before the end of the century they were working as lawyers, doctors, journalists, civil servants, secretaries, and in a variety of other white-collar and professional occupations.

Most women did not share the deep sense of grievance that led the feminists to launch their crusade against male tyranny. Neither the law and custom governing family relationships, nor the state of women's opportunities for education and employment, were matters of great importance to the majority of women who were not tyrannized by men and had no ambitions for careers. The ranks of feminism were drawn mainly from the relatively well-educated, well-to-do in the urban East and Middle West. It

was in this segment of the population that women w
most likely to feel caught between the genteel opposit....
to women's employment, on the one hand, and, on the
other, new opportunities and new ideas about women's
place in life.

The importance of these attitudes toward women's employment cannot be measured in terms of the small numbers who endorsed one extreme view or the other. People
on all social and economic levels were influenced, to a degree, by the attitudes and ideas of both sides. The extent
of antagonism toward the employment of women is best
illustrated by the fact that almost all women retired from
work when they married. Even in families which thought
nothing of sending young girls to factories, married women
rarely worked. One reason, of course, was that most wives
were so busy at home. But even among those who did not
have young children to care for or much else to do, very
few worked. Once a girl assumed the full status of womanhood, she automatically stayed home.

The influence of feminists also extended far beyond feminist circles. Their controversy with conservatives was important just because it took place among the relatively well-
educated, well-to-do minority. The daughters of the poor
had always worked outside the home wherever unskilled
manual jobs were available. The feminists raised a new
question about a different group of women: were the abilities of women who had more to offer than unskilled labor
to be used only in the home, or were they to be used as
well in the performance of a wide variety of tasks in the
outside world? This, in turn, raised fundamental questions
about the education of women, for it was clear that their
potentialities could not be realized unless women had a

chance to develop them through education. And it was equally plain that if women were educated, some of them would want to use their training outside the home.

No one can say just how much the feminists contributed to broadening educational and economic opportunities for women. They had on their side not only the growth of the industrial economy, but the trend toward democracy which dominated much of the history of the Western world during the nineteenth century. In any event, the feminist program did make progress. Though few women were interested in careers, the path for those who were was much easier by the close of the century than it had been only a decade or two earlier.

The echoes of the nineteenth-century woman's movement have not ceased even today. There is still, for instance, a National Woman's Party dedicated to the overthrow of the legal bastions of male tyranny. By the end of World War I, however, both the feminist movement and the controversies it stirred up were rapidly subsiding. The climate in the twenties was strikingly different from that of the prewar decades. By 1920 women had already won a great deal of what they had been striving for. The Eighteenth and Nineteenth Amendments, establishing prohibition and granting women the vote, both went into effect in 1920. Every student of the period agrees that the role played by women in the war led to a remarkable liberalization of views about women's abilities and the propriety of their working outside the home.

Yet women seemed strangely disinterested during the twenties in some of the victories they had worked so hard to gain. The daughters of the suffragettes showed little interest in politics, and some of the daughters of temperance advocates seemed interested mainly in demonstrating their capacity for bootleg gin. The proportion of women working for pay increased almost imperceptibly, and the vast majority of women continued to retire from work when they married. Young women seemed indifferent to their now established right to obtain professional training. The militant feminist approach to careers as the main hope of fulfillment faded into obscurity, and there were no significant increases during the twenties in the employment of women in professions other than teaching and nursing.

What might appear as mere fickleness becomes understandable if it is recalled that the feminists were never more than a small minority, and that women had already established their primary claim to equal status and dignity. Moreover, like the suffrage and temperance movements, the economic demands of feminism were motivated largely by the desire to protect women against the abuse of masculine prerogatives. Consequently, each of these demands became less important as the special privileges of men were limited, and as the climate of attitudes shifted toward recognition of the essential equality of women.

By the twenties the personal and property rights of women under law had been greatly enlarged. Liberalization of divorce law by judicial interpretation as well as by statute made it much easier for a woman to escape from an unsatisfactory marriage—with alimony. Underlying these legal developments were changes in values and attitudes so extensive that it is difficult for the post-World War I generation to grasp what it was like to be a woman in the prewar decades. These changes were reflected in the careers of Helen Wills and Gertrude Ederle, the first women to become national sports idols. They were caricatured in the popular image of the flapper, who smoked, drank, and enjoyed the same freedom of social intercourse as men. That the flapper was often a "coed" was one sign of the growing acceptance of higher education for women. Even more fundamental were the changes that took place in sexual attitudes. The flapper costume, with its short skirts and flat bosom, might be construed as a symbolic emphasis on women's sexual functions at the expense of the maternal. In any case, the twenties did bring a franker acknowledgment of sex, and a first admission that women had sexual needs as well as maternal instincts.

Knowledge and approval of birth-control methods spread rapidly during the twenties, especially among the middle classes. The birth rate, which had been falling for at least a hundred years, continued to decline. Even before the onset of the depression, it was far below the prewar level, and the number of two-child, one-child, and no-child marriages had increased sharply. At the same time the physical and emotional burdens of raising children were steadily reduced by improvements in medical care, and infant mortality continued to fall sharply. It was not until the twenties, moreover, that the electrical revolution in home technology got well under way.

In short, the decade after World War I witnessed a sharp and many-sided equalization of both the public and private status of women, together with a substantial reduction of the perils and burdens of marriage and maternity. These developments had a double significance. They removed the edge from the feminist desire to seek in paid work a way of asserting equality. At the same time, however, they helped to reduce the obstacles to women's employment, and so smoothed the way for the developments of the next three decades.

The most obvious effect of the depression of the 1930's was to throw many women out of work and to intensify the feeling that working women took jobs away from male breadwinners. Many state and local governments revived old bans on the employment of married women in teaching and other public jobs, and several state legislatures considered bills to prohibit the employment of wives in private industry. But the depression of the thirties, like that of the nineties, also had another and perhaps more lasting effect. A great many women who would not have thought of working in normal times took whatever odd jobs they could get to help replace income lost because husbands, fathers, and brothers were unemployed. In spite of the scarcity of jobs, the female labor force appears to have grown more rapidly between 1930 and 1940 than it had in either of the two previous decades.

By 1940 the proportion of married women in the labor force was several times greater than it had been at the turn of the century. Nevertheless, the overwhelming majority of young women still retired from work when they married. The principal change in attitudes toward women's employment was reflected in the fact that most single women from the upper social and economic levels now worked. The general case against women's employment had become a specific case against the employment of wives and mothers.

When depression gave way to war, jobs again became plentiful. Families which had struggled for ten years suddenly found that there was work for all. Public opinion polls during the war showed that many men and women still felt that women belonged home. On the other hand, women were now told that it was their patriotic duty to take a job, and millions of them went to work: rich and poor; young, middle-aged, and old; single, married, widowed, and divorced. The war affected the attitudes of employers too. Faced with severe shortages of male workers, many employers quickly revised their notions of what jobs women could and should hold.

At the end of the war most people anticipated a severe wave of unemployment, and believed that the married women who had taken jobs should go back home. Many of them did in 1946 and 1947, even though the postwar depression failed to materialize, but many others stayed at work. In the prosperous years that followed the number of young people entering the labor force was much below normal because of the low birth rates of the thirties. As the demand for labor grew, the number of wives and mothers in the labor force began to increase again and has continued to rise ever since, especially among the well-educated and relatively well-to-do.

This increase was not even halted by the relatively severe recession of 1957–58. Among married women in their thirties, forties, and fifties, the proportion in the labor force continued to grow throughout 1957 and the first half of 1958. Mainly because fewer teen-aged girls and elderly women were working or looking for work, the proportion of all women in the labor force did not increase during most of 1957. During the first half of 1958, however, the long-run trend was resumed. By June, 1958, the number of women in the labor force reached 23 million for the first time. Of all women over fourteen, 37 percent were working or looking for work, the highest figure on record for that month. Even though unemployment was also increasing, more women were actually working in 1957 and the first six months of 1958 than in any preceding year.

A great deal of concern was expressed in 1890 over the presence in the labor force of some 4 million women, most of them single. Since World War II, however, the decision of millions of middle-aged, middle-class wives and mothers to go to work has caused little alarm. It is now permissible for any woman to work. She may not have the full approval of her church, her neighbors, or her family, especially if she has young children. But neither will she meet with general opprobrium, even if she has young children, as long as she provides adequate substitute care. To understand this contrast it is helpful to recall again that the opposition to women's employment in 1890 stemmed largely from the fear that it constituted one among several dangerous threats to the stability of the family and the well-being of society. Today's acceptance of the married working woman suggests that such fears have long since been alleviated.

American women have shown by their behavior during the last two decades that they value their role in the family far above their role in the labor force. As the proportion of women in the labor force has gone up, the average age at marriage has gone down; the proportion of women remaining single has fallen; and the birth rate has increased spectacularly. Most working wives have waited until their children were in school before they returned to work; and as long as their children are young, they usually work part time or intermittently.

Most of today's working wives show no strong internal commitment to work. They work for a variety of reasons—including the need to feel useful and important—but they work mainly in order to earn money they don't absolutely have to have. In this respect, they resemble the majority of single women who worked in 1890, rather than the career-minded minority. By contrast with many of the working girls of 1890, however, today's working wives are less likely to be working so that they can be independent, more likely to be working to better the circumstances of their families. The fact that the recent recession did not revive the old argument that women take jobs away from men suggests how far Americans have gone toward accepting women's earnings as a normal part of family support.

Nineteenth-century fears about the impact of women's employment upon the social order have also been relieved. The pre-World War I type of feminist, who boasted that through work women would upset the whole existing pattern of relationships between the sexes, has all but disappeared. Americans have now had time to grow accustomed to the greater freedom and more equal status of women, and to recognize that these developments do not lead to social catastrophe. In any event, these changes have been so far-reaching that no sensible person could hope to halt or reverse them by limiting the employment of women. To argue, for instance, that immoral behavior is stimulated by the proximity of young men and women at work would be pointless today in view of such developments as the spread of coeducation and the general freedom of social contact enjoyed by both sexes.

This is not to say that none of the old issues remains, or that all of the old attitudes have disappeared. Prevailing conceptions of the fundamental qualities of men and women have changed enormously, but some have showed great persistence. One student wrote, a few years ago, that "psychologists and sociologists are now agreed that there are no significant differences between the sexes in intellectual capacity, in personality traits, in citizenship responsibilities, or in spiritual and personal needs." [42] Actually, there is still a great deal of scholarly controversy over all of these items except intellectual capacity. Whatever the scholars may have concluded, a good many nineteenth-century ideas about women's special attributes are still widely accepted. In 1946, for instance, a *Fortune* poll showed a plurality of both sexes agreeing that women have less ability to handle people well, to make decisions, and to create or invent. The largest numbers of respondents also believed that women are less even-tempered, less selfish, more extravagant, and more polite than men.[43]

The continuing debate over the proper kind of higher education for women still turns on the effort to define their essential qualities. This is true of many of those who argue for more emphasis on liberal arts or on vocational training as well as those who stress preparation for homemaking and family life. Even when it is assumed that there are no innate differences, it is commonly argued that the education of women must be adapted to the unique qualities imposed upon them by their culturally assigned functions. A few years ago, for instance, the male president of a well-known woman's college acknowledged that "women can succeed in practically any profession men enter." Nevertheless, he found that woman should prepare herself to perform those "functions in her society which she may and should exercise by virtue of the fact that she is a

woman." Among the special female functions, he included
the following: spending the family's income, nurturing the
liberal and fine arts, educating the young, preserving re-
ligion, and reforming society. Because of these, and other
unique female needs, he concluded that women should
attend women's colleges and should pursue a basic liberal
arts program especially adapted to their "expected use of it,"
their interests, and their "typical idiom." [44]

Today, as in 1890, most people believe that women have
special qualifications and special handicaps for particular
kinds of work. The modern champions of women's rights
advance much the same demand as the feminists of the late
nineteenth century: equal opportunity to develop and utilize the special qualities of women. Thus, Margaret Mead
points out that every known society maintains artificial
occupational divisions and personality expectations that limit
the humanity of the other sex. But she also suspects that
"there are certain fields, such as the physical sciences, mathematics, and instrumental music, in which men . . . will
always have that razor-edge of extra gift which makes all
the difference." And what she asks for is "freedom to admit
freely and cultivate in each sex their special superiorities." [45]
One woman executive has expressed a similar viewpoint in
these words: "I like being a woman. My attitude is that I
can contribute something as a woman. I'm not as self-con-
scious about warmth as a man would be. My reaction is
much more emotional—and emotion is a necessary com-
modity. There are places where I can't fill the bill as well as
a man, and I don't try." [46]

Attitudes such as these still influence women's preparation for work and the jobs they hold. Girls begin to learn
at an early age that they are not expected to show an in-

terest in mathematics, the sciences, or technical subjects. By the time they reach adolescence most girls expect to work when they leave school, but, insofar as they view their education as preparation for work, the overwhelming majority turn to such traditionally female occupations as teaching, nursing, or secretarial work. If a girl shows any tendency to enter a less traditional field, she is likely to meet with skepticism, if not opposition, from friends, parents, teachers, and even guidance counselors. When the 2,675 girl high school seniors in suburban Nassau County, New York, were questioned in 1954, all but 138 said that they expected to go to work when they completed their formal education. Nearly two thirds were planning to become teachers, nurses, or office workers. Only 74 girls hoped to become managers or executives, and 61 of these wanted to be buyers.[47] Most employers share the same narrow outlook on women's jobs. The universal division of help-wanted columns into male and female sections illustrates the fact that employers still specify one sex or the other in filling jobs. Only occasionally does the same entry appear under both headings.

Ideas about male and female qualities still have a profound impact, not only on where and how women work, but also on whether or not they work at all outside the home. There is a strong tendency in psychiatric literature to reaffirm the old view that paid employment is antagonistic to woman's immutable emotional needs.[48] Women who work, according to this viewpoint, are sure to compromise both their own femininity and their husbands' masculinity, and to arouse deep conflicts and anxieties in the process. Many psychiatrists dissent from these views, but whether or not they are scientifically valid, there is no question that many women do not work because they, or their husbands, are convinced that the home is woman's natural environment. It is also clear that similar feelings produce a great deal of tension in many families where the wife does work.

While these older issues still receive a good deal of attention, the focus of controversy over women's work has shifted in recent years. As more and more wives and mothers have entered the labor force, arguments about woman's nature have been replaced, to a large extent, by discussion of the conflicting demands of home and work upon the time and energy of women.[49]

It is commonly asserted, for instance, that the employment of mothers is largely responsible for reported increases in juvenile delinquency. While not going this far, many psychiatrists, social workers, and church leaders maintain that the emotional development of children is endangered when mothers spend time at work rather than at home. Abram Kardiner, for instance, has written that "children reared on a spare-time basis will show the effects of such care in the distortions of character that inevitably result. Motherhood is a full-time job. . . ."[50] Supporters of this view generally agree, however, that children are no longer endangered by their mother's absence once they reach a certain age, which has been set as low as three and as high as eighteen.

The most conspicuous feature of contemporary discussion of this problem is the paucity of evidence, and the preponderance of theory and assumption. There is very little knowledge about how children react when they are separated from their mothers for part of each day, or about how this reaction is affected by other circumstances.

Moreover, the many other ways in which family relationships are affected when the mother works have been virtually ignored.

Similarly, the effect of women's home responsibilities upon their performance and upon their opportunities on the job has aroused a great deal of heated speculation, but very little study. Employers continue to assume that women workers are unreliable, that they stay home or quit their jobs when their families need them, that they have little initiative or ambition, but there have been very few studies of how men and women actually behave in different kinds of jobs.[51]

Likewise, little attention has been paid to the educational and training needs of women who come back to work after a long interval as full-time housewives. Indeed, there is hardly any information about the work histories of individual women. It is not known, for instance, how many work all their adult lives, how many quit to take care of children and never return, how long those who return have been away from work, whether they come back to the same or different kinds of work, or what specific problems of adjustment, learning, or re-learning they encounter. The authors of a recent study of "women's two roles" were astonished to find

that in this era of social investigations so little systematic research has been done on the vital problems concerning women in contemporary society. Tremendous changes in their way of life, and in their position in the family and society have taken place during the life-time of the present generation. We are, in fact, the unobservant participants of a social revolution. . . . On practically each point in the discussion we have had to look in vain for evidence that had been scientifically collected and examined.[52]

A great deal has been written in the last decade about the conflict between women's employment and their home responsibilities, but most of it has been devoted to angry expression of the resentment and frustration some women have experienced as the result of their desire to achieve success and satisfaction in work without neglecting their responsibilities to their families. This dilemma, of course, is a new one. When the economy was based on agriculture and domestic industry, there was not much of a problem in reconciling home and work. Men, women, and children all worked, and all of the activities of each, including work, were centered in the home. But since the modern economy is based on specialization, it exerts a strong centrifugal influence on the family, whose members find that they can achieve many of their goals more fully or more efficiently outside the family circle.

The nineteenth-century case against women's employment sought to keep them in a home that was increasingly deprived of vital activities and the presence of other adults. This effort, which never succeeded completely, is now being abandoned as more and more women join their brothers, fathers, and husbands in work outside the home. The separation of home and work is one of the dominant features of modern life and it creates similar problems for both sexes. The woman who sacrifices success in a career so that she may raise her children properly has much in common with the man who limits his chances for promotion by spending evenings and week ends with his family rather than in his office.

The revolution in women's work since the close of the last century is inseparably linked with a long series of changes in the character of the economy, the nature of work, the shape of American society, the life of the family, and even in the prevailing image of what it means to be a man or a woman. This study has stressed the causes rather than the momentous consequences of changes in women's work. By taking a new place in the economy, women have helped to transform the face of America during the first half of the twentieth century. It would be foolhardy to predict the pattern of developments in the years ahead. One may be certain, however, that the rapidly increasing employment of wives and mothers since the outbreak of World War II will leave a deep imprint on every side of American life during the second half of the century.

Appendix

A NOTE ON
STATISTICS

THE ONLY SOURCE of comprehensive data on the number of working women and their occupations is the U.S. Census. Before 1940 the Census counted those persons, aged ten years and over, who were "gainfully occupied." A gainfully occupied person was defined, essentially, as one who pursued with some regularity an activity which produced money income. Since 1940 the Census has counted persons in the "labor force," which is a much more precise approach. The labor force includes all persons aged fourteen and over who work for pay or profit for any length of time during a given week or who seek such work; and those who work for fifteen hours a week or more in a profit-making family enterprise, even if not paid.

The reader who wishes an analysis and summary of the data on women's employment may consult National Manpower Council, *Womanpower* (New York, 1957), Chapters II and IV. The data are presented in more detail in such standard works as Alba M. Edwards, *Comparative Occupation Statistics for the United States, 1870 to 1940* (Washington, 1943); David L. Kaplan and M. Claire Casey, *Occupational Trends in the United States, 1900 to 1950*, Bureau of the Census Working Paper No. 5 (Washington, 1958); John D. Durand, *The Labor Force in the United States, 1890–1960* (New York, 1948); Gertrude Bancroft, *The American Labor Force: Its Growth and Changing Composition* (New York, 1958); Janet M. Hooks, *Women's Occupations through Seven Decades*, U.S. Women's Bureau Bulletin No. 218 (Washington, 1947); U.S. Women's Bureau

Bulletin No. 253, *Changes in Women's Occupations, 1940–1950* (Washington, 1954).

Comparison of Census data on women's employment in different years must be undertaken with extreme caution. The definition of a gainfully occupied person was much narrower in 1890 than in later years. The 1890 Census counted a person as gainfully occupied only if he reported an occupation "upon which he chiefly depends for support, and in which he would ordinarily be engaged during the larger part of the year." This definition excluded most of the large number of women who earned money through homework and many of those who worked irregularly away from home. In addition, a great many who qualified under the definition were not counted. Because most women did not work regularly for pay, and because the Census instructions emphasized the circumstances under which women should not be counted as gainfully occupied, Census takers were likely to be careless in recording women's work. This tendency was reinforced by the *ad hoc* character of the Census organization and by the tendency of respondents to reflect prevailing views of women's proper role by concealing the employment of female members of the family. As a result of all these circumstances, any woman who was both a housekeeper and a paid worker, or a student and a paid worker, was likely to be recorded only as a housekeeper or student.

It is particularly important to keep this in mind when evaluating analyses of long-term trends in women's work. The increasing employment of women shown by the Census data reflects not only the growing employment of women for pay, but also the growing willingness of respondents to report women's work, the broadening of Census definitions, improvement of the Census organization and procedures, and the decline of homework, which could be more easily overlooked than work away from home. The Census has never sought to distinguish between women who work for pay inside the home and those employed outside. Nevertheless, because very few women now qualify as members of the labor force through home employment, the labor force data may be used to approximate the number of women now working for pay outside the home.

Although the data for recent years are much more precise and, on the whole, more inclusive than the data for 1930 and earlier years, there is still some question about the accuracy of the Census count of women workers. Some members of the labor force inevitably escape enumeration. It is generally acknowledged that this is most likely to happen when counting women and children who work irregularly, especially if they are unpaid workers on a family farm or in a family business.

The occupational and demographic data which appear in the text without source citations are drawn from the following Census publications:

Report on the Population of the United States at the Eleventh Census: 1890 (2 vols.)

U.S. Census of Population: 1950
    Vol. II. Characteristics of the Population
    Vol. IV. Special Reports

Current Population Reports
    Series P–20: Population Characteristics
        P–50: Labor Force
        P–57: Monthly Report on the Labor Force
        P–60: Consumer Income

NOTES

CHAPTER I: THE WORK OF WOMEN

1. All data on the number of working women and their occupations which appear without specific source citation are derived from U.S. Census reports. For an explanation and evaluation of these data, see the Appendix which precedes these notes.

2. Mary Austin, *Earth Horizon: Autobiography* (Boston and New York, 1932), p. 115.

3. William Blackstone, *Commentaries on the Laws of England* (American Student's Edition, prepared by George Chase, New York, 1877), p. 154.

4. Cited in Matilda Gage, *Woman, Church, and State* (New York, 1893), pp. 390–91.

5. Arthur W. Calhoun, *A Social History of the American Family* (Cleveland, 1919), III, 111.

6. Charles W. Marsh, *Recollections, 1837–1910* (Chicago, 1910), p. 298.

7. John Ise, *Sod and Stubble* (New York, 1940).

8. Willa Cather, *My Ántonia* (Cambridge, Mass., 1926), pp. 199–200.

9. Langley Porter, *A New Jersey Farm Then and Now* (mimeographed, 1937), pp. 2–3, 9–10.

10. Mrs. Emma Haddock, "Women as Land-Owners in the West," *Papers Read before the Association for the Advancement of Women, 14th Women's Congress*, Louisville, October, 1886, p. 24.

11. U.S. Commissioner of Labor, *Sixth Annual Report: Cost of Production* (Washington, 1891), pp. 693 ff.

12. Peter Roberts, *Anthracite Coal Communities* (New York, 1904), p. 107.

13. Arthur M. Schlesinger, *The Rise of the City: 1878–1898* (New York, 1938), p. 84.

14. U.S. Commissioner of Labor, *Sixth Annual Report*, pp. 693 ff.; *Seventh Annual Report: Cost of Production* (Washington, 1892), pp. 866 ff.; U.S. Senate, Committee on Finance, *Retail Prices and Wages*, The Aldrich Report (Washington, 1892), pp. 2060–63.

15. Maude Nathan, *Once Upon a Time and Today* (New York, 1933), pp. 83 ff., 107.

16. Paul C. Glick, *American Families* (New York, 1957), p. 11.

17. U.S. Commissioner of Labor, *Sixth Annual Report*, pp. 693 ff.; *Seventh Annual Report*, pp. 866 ff.; U.S. Senate, Committee on Finance, *Retail Prices and Wages*, pp. 2048–51.

18. R. C. Chapin, "The Influence of Income on Standards of Life," *American Journal of Sociology*, XIV (1909), 646.

19. Mrs. John Van Vorst and Marie Van Vorst, *The Woman Who Toils* (New York, 1903), pp. 67–68.

20. Gilson Willets, *Workers of the Nation* (New York, 1903), I, 302–3.

21. New York State, Legislature, *Report and Testimony Taken before the Special Committee of the Assembly Appointed to Investigate the Condition of Female Labor in the City of New York* (Albany, 1896), pp. 854–55.

22. *Ibid.*, pp. 15–16, 919–22.

23. Frances A. Kellor, *Out of Work: A Study of Employment Agencies* (New York, 1904), p. 35.

24. Alice H. Rhine, "Women in Industry," in Annie N. Meyer, ed., *Woman's Work in America* (New York, 1891), pp. 296–98.

25. For an excellent review of the early history of women's employment in American industry, see Edith Abbott, *Women in Industry* (New York, 1909).

26. Elizabeth B. Butler, *Women and the Trades, Pittsburgh, 1907–08*, The Pittsburgh Survey (New York, 1911), p. 227.

27. U.S. Commissioner of Labor, *Fourth Annual Report:*

Working Women in Large Cities (Washington, 1889), pp. 62–64.

28. "Women as Teachers," *Educational Review*, II (1891), 361.

29. Kate V. Wofford, *An History of the Status and Training of Elementary Rural Teachers, 1860–1930* (New York, 1935), p. 34.

30. Willard S. Elsbree, *The American Teacher: Evolution of a Profession in a Democracy* (New York, 1939), p. 321.

31. Mary M. Roberts, *American Nursing: History and Interpretation* (New York, 1954), pp. 5, 28.

32. Mary P. Jacobi, "Woman in Medicine" in Meyer, ed., *Woman's Work in America*, pp. 139 ff.

33. Ada M. Bittenbender, "Woman in Law," *ibid.*, pp. 218 ff.

34. N.Y. State, Legislature, *Condition of Female Labor in the City of New York*, pp. 255–57.

35. Glick, *American Families*, p. 11.

36. Robert H. Bremner, *From the Depths: The Discovery of Poverty in the United States* (New York, 1956), p. 52.

37. Lorine P. Fryer, *Women and Leisure* (New York, 1924), pp. vii, 6.

38. Nathan, *Once Upon a Time and Today*, p. 85.

39. U.S. Department of the Interior, Census Office, *Report on Population of the United States at the Eleventh Census: 1890*, Part II (Washington, 1897), pp. lxxvii–lxxviii.

40. Schlesinger, *The Rise of the City*, pp. 143–44.

41. U.S. Office of Education, *Biennial Survey of Education in the United States, 1951–52*, Ch. 2 (Washington, 1955), p. 25.

CHAPTER II: THE WOMEN WHO WORK

1. Nathan, *Once Upon a Time and Today*, p. 45.

2. Katherine G. Busbey, *Home Life in America* (New York, 1910), pp. 135–36.

3. Van Vorst, *The Woman Who Toils*, pp. 68, 82, 159.

4. *Ibid.*, pp. 131–32, 173–74.

5. Frank H. Streightoff, *The Standard of Living among the Industrial People of America* (Boston and New York, 1911), pp. 97–98.

6. Collected in Helen Campbell, *Prisoners of Poverty* (Boston, 1877), pp. 18–29.

7. N.Y. State, Legislature, *Condition of Female Labor in the City of New York*, pp. 603–5.

8. Van Vorst, *The Woman Who Toils*, pp. 283–85.

9. For examples see Clarence D. Long, *Labor Force, Income, and Employment* (mimeographed, National Bureau of Economic Research, 1950), Ch. V.

10. U.S. Commissioner of Labor, *Fourth Annual Report: Working Women in Large Cities*, pp. 18–19.

11. Margaret F. Byington, "The Family in a Typical Mill Town," *American Journal of Sociology*, XIV (1909), 649–50.

12. Holland Thompson, "The Southern Textile Situation," *South Atlantic Quarterly*, April, 1930, p. 115.

13. Broadus Mitchell, and G. S. Mitchell, *The Industrial Revolution in the South* (Baltimore, 1930), p. 10.

14. U.S. Commissioner of Labor, *Fourth Annual Report*, p. 73.

15. U.S. Office of Education, *Biennial Survey, 1951–52*, Ch. 5 (Washington, 1954), p. 6.

16. Lotus D. Coffman, *The Social Composition of the Teaching Population* (New York, 1911), p. 80.

17. Christine L. Franklin, "The Education of Woman in the Southern States" in Meyer, ed., *Woman's Work in America*, p. 106.

18. U.S. Office of Education, *Biennial Survey, 1951–52*, Ch. 1 (Washington, 1955), p. 40.

19. U.S. Bureau of Labor Statistics, Bulletin 175, *Summary of the Report on Conditions of Women and Child Wage Earners in the United States* (Washington, 1916), pp. 163–64.

20. Bremner, *From the Depths*, p. 222.

21. W. S. Woytinsky and E. S. Woytinsky, *World Population and Production* (New York, 1953), pp. 203 ff.

22. Robert Hunter, *Poverty* (New York, 1912), pp. 36–37; U.S. Bureau of the Census, *Historical Statistics of the United States* (Washington, 1949), p. 154.

23. North Carolina Bureau of Labor Statistics, *Fifth Annual Report, 1891* (Raleigh, 1892), p. 169.

24. Austin, *Earth Horizon*, pp. 91–92.

25. W. Jett Lauck and Edgar Sydenstricker, *Conditions of Labor in American Industries* (New York, 1917), p. 208.

26. Van Vorst, *The Woman Who Toils*, pp. 269, 283.

27. U.S. Commissioner of Labor, *Eighteenth Annual Report: Cost of Living and Retail Prices of Food* (Washington, 1904), p. 44.

28. Paul Douglas, *Real Wages* (Boston and New York, 1930), p. 445.

29. U.S. Commissioner of Labor, *Seventh Special Report: The Slums of Baltimore, Chicago, New York, and Philadelphia* (Washington, 1894), p. 52.

30. U.S. Commissioner of Labor, *Seventh Annual Report: Cost of Production*, pp. 879–80, 957–58.

31. Glick, *American Families*, p. 54.

32. See Donald J. Bogue, "Urbanism in the United States, 1950," *American Journal of Sociology*, LX (1955), 471–86.

33. These developments are analysed in Herman P. Miller, *Income of the American People* (New York, 1955).

34. See National Manpower Council, *Work in the Lives of Married Women* (New York, 1958), pp. 136, 191–93.

35. These and other changes in the opportunities of Negroes are discussed in Eli Ginzberg (assisted by James K. Anderson, Douglas W. Bray, and Robert W. Smuts), *The Negro Potential* (New York, 1956).

CHAPTER III: THE DEMANDS AND REWARDS OF WOMEN'S WORK

1. N.Y. State, Legislature, *Condition of Female Labor in the City of New York*, pp. 272, 602, 691.

2. Van Vorst, *The Woman Who Toils*, pp. 181–82, 222.

3. Dorothy Richardson, *The Long Day: The True Story of a New York Working Girl as Told by Herself* (New York, 1905), pp. 231–33 and *passim*.

4. Kellor, *Out of Work*, Ch. 1–4, *passim*.

5. *Ibid.*, pp. 215 ff.

6. Elsbree, *The American Teacher*, pp. 340, 473; Wofford,

History of the Status and Training of Elementary Rural Teachers, pp. 28 ff.

7. Isabel M. Stewart, *The Education of Nurses, Historical Foundations and Modern Trends* (New York, 1943), pp. 124–30, 141.

8. Theodore Dreiser, *Sister Carrie* (Sagamore Press edition, New York, 1957), pp. 31 ff.

9. Van Vorst, *The Woman Who Toils*, pp. 22 ff.

10. Richardson, *The Long Day*, pp. 71, 204, 236, 243.

11. Lewis Mumford, *Technics and Civilization* (New York, 1934), pp. 224–25.

12. Robert W. Smuts, *European Impressions of the American Worker* (New York, 1953), pp. 22–23.

13. New Jersey Bureau of Statistics of Labor and Industries, *Tenth Annual Report* (Somerville, N.J., 1888), pp. 203–4.

14. Willets, *Workers of the Nation*, I, 487–88.

15. Daniel Pidgeon, *Old World Questions and New World Answers* (London, 1884), pp. 40–41.

16. Butler, *Women and the Trades*, p. 314.

17. Van Vorst, *The Woman Who Toils*, pp. 27–28, 159, and *passim*.

18. Nathan, *Once Upon a Time and Today*, p. 81.

19. Minnie Goodnow, *Nursing History* (Philadelphia, 1953), p. 197.

20. Adelaide M. Nutting and Lavinia L. Dock, *A History of Nursing* (New York, 1907–12), II, 117. See also Linda Richards, *Reminiscences of America's First Trained Nurse* (Boston, 1911).

21. U.S. Office of Education, *Biennial Survey of Education in the United States, 1949–50*, Ch. 2 (Washington, 1952), p. 19.

22. Fred A. Shannon, *The Farmer's Last Frontier* (New York, 1945), pp. 372 ff.

23. Anon., *The Autobiography of a Happy Woman* (New York, 1914), pp. 63 ff.

24. Bruce Bliven, Jr., *The Wonderful Writing Machine* (New York, 1954), pp. 6–8.

25. Dreiser, *Sister Carrie*, pp. 31–32.

26. Richardson, *The Long Day*, pp. 204–5.

27. Van Vorst, *The Woman Who Toils*, p. 117.

28. Campbell, *Prisoners of Poverty*, p. 180.

29. See, for instance, Roberts, *Anthracite Coal Communities;* Herbert J. Lahne, *The Cotton Mill Worker* (New York, 1944); Jennings Rhyne, *Some Southern Cotton Mill Workers and Their Villages* (Chapel Hill, 1930).

30. New York *Times*, Aug. 21, 1902.

31. Calhoun, *American Family*, III, 209.

32. Pidgeon, *Old World Questions and New World Answers*, pp. 231, 234.

33. Elsbree, *The American Teacher*, pp. 355, 473-74.

34. Richardson, *The Long Day*, p. 243.

35. Rhine, "Women in Industry" in Meyer, ed., *Woman's Work in America*, p. 291.

36. U.S. Commissioner of Labor, *Fourth Annual Report: Working Women in Large Cities*, p. 76.

37. See, for instance, Helen Campbell, *Women Wage Earners* (Boston, 1893), pp. 220-21; Maude Nathan, *The Story of an Epoch-Making Movement* (New York, 1926), pp. 7-8.

38. Data on wages are contained in most of the sources already cited. Collected data on the earnings of large numbers of women in various cities and occupations may be found in the reports of the U.S. Commissioner of Labor. See especially *Fourth Annual Report: Working Women in Large Cities*, pp. 484-531; *Seventh Special Report: The Slums of Baltimore, Chicago, New York, and Philadelphia*, pp. 212-501; *Eleventh Annual Report: Work and Wages of Men, Women, and Children* (Washington, 1897), pp. 35-513.

39. Nathan, *An Epoch-Making Movement*, pp. 26-27.

40. Stewart, *Education of Nurses*, p. 97; Goodnow, *Nursing History*, p. 197; Roberts, *American Nursing*, p. 3.

41. U.S. Commissioner of Labor, *Eleventh Annual Report*, pp. 11, 28.

42. W. Randolph Burgess, *Trends of School Costs* (New York, 1920), p. 33. See also Wofford, *History of the Status and Training of Elementary Rural Teachers*, pp. 42 ff.

43. Herbert J. Lahne, Labor in the Cotton Mill, 1865-1900 (unpublished master's essay, Columbia University, 1937), pp. 196-97.

44. Richardson, *The Long Day*, pp. 151 ff.

45. U.S. Commissioner of Labor, *Fourth Annual Report*, p. 625.

46. Campbell, *Prisoners of Poverty*, pp. 120–22.

47. N.Y. State, Legislature, *Condition of Female Labor in the City of New York*, pp. 1097–1100, 1175–76.

48. N.C. Bureau of Labor Statistics, *Fifth Annual Report*, pp. 175, 194, 195.

49. Collected in Campbell, *Prisoners of Poverty*.

50. Richardson, *The Long Day*, pp. 302–3.

51. J. F. Dewhurst, *America's Needs and Resources* (New York, 1955), p. 732.

52. U.S. Bureau of Labor Statistics, Report 100, *Trends in Output per Man-Hour and Man-Hours per Unit of Output—Manufacturing, 1939–53* (Washington, 1955), p. 34.

53. The relationship between economic development and the skills of the work force is discussed more fully in National Manpower Council, *A Policy for Skilled Manpower* (New York, 1954), especially Ch. 1.

54. Roberts, *American Nursing*, p. 286; Stewart, *Education of Nurses*, p. 246.

CHAPTER IV: WOMEN, MEN, AND WORK: VALUES AND ATTITUDES

1. *Reports of Cases Argued and Determined in the Supreme Court of the State of Wisconsin*, XXXIX (Chicago, 1876), 245.

2. Julia Ward Howe, "Opening Address," *Papers, Association for Advancement of Women, 15th Congress* (New York, October, 1887), p. 9.

3. "Woman in Medicine" in Meyer, ed., *Woman's Work in America*, pp. 176–77.

4. Charlotte Perkins Gilman, *Women and Economics* (Boston, 1898), pp. 31 ff.

5. Edward H. Clarke, *Sex in Education* (5th edition, Boston, 1874), pp. 33, 47–48.

6. Azel Ames, *Sex in Industry* (Boston, 1875), *passim*.

7. Massachusetts Bureau of Statistics of Labor, *Sixteenth Annual Report* (Boston, 1885), p. 517.

8. Grant Allen, "Woman's Place in Nature," *The Forum*, VII, 263.

9. Calhoun, *American Family*, III, 91.

10. *Reports, Supreme Court of Wisconsin*, XXXIX, 245–46.

11. Willets, *Workers of the Nation*, II, 934–35.

12. G. Ferrers, "The Law of Non Labor," *Literary Digest*, VIII (Feb. 1, 1894), 308–9.

13. Laura Clay, "Woman's Suffrage Symposium," *Papers, Association for Advancement of Women, 14th Congress*, p. 119.

14. Ames, *Sex in Industry*, pp. 30–31.

15. Ferrers, "The Law of Non Labor," *Literary Digest*, VIII (Feb. 1, 1894), 308.

16. U.S. Commissioner of Labor, *Eleventh Annual Report*, pp. 11, 21.

17. Van Vorst, *The Woman Who Toils*, pp. 54, 55, 160–63.

18. See, for instance, Abbott, *Women in Industry, passim;* Mabel Hurd Willett, *The Employment of Women in the Clothing Trade* (New York, 1902), pp. 54–72; Butler, *Women and the Trades*, pp. 342–44 and *passim*.

19. Anon., *Autobiography of a Happy Woman*, pp. 215–16.

20. Austin, *Earth Horizon*, p. 280.

21. *Truth* (San Francisco), Jan. 26, 1884, quoted in Calhoun, *American Family*, III, 324.

22. Rebecca N. Hazard, "Home Studies for Women," *Papers, Association for Advancement of Women, 15th Congress*, pp. 17–24.

23. Frances E. Willard and Mary A. Livermore, *A Woman of the Century: Biographical Sketches of Leading American Women* (Buffalo, 1893), pp. 367–68.

24. Jacobi, "Woman in Medicine" in Meyer, ed., *Woman's Work in America*, p. 197.

25. Bittenbender, "Woman in Law," *ibid.*, p. 228.

26. *Association for the Advancement of Women, Thirteenth Annual Report, Woman's Congress* (Des Moines, 1885), p. 15.

27. *Ibid.*, *16th Woman's Congress* (Detroit, 1888), pp. 60 ff.

28. "Opening Address," *ibid.*, *14th Congress*, p. 9.

29. The Vice Commission of Chicago, *The Social Evil in Chicago* (Chicago, 1911), pp. 199, 261–63.

30. See Charlotte Perkins Gilman, *The Home, Its Work and Influence* (New York, 1903).

31. See, for instance, William Cole and Florett Robinson, eds., *Women are Wonderful: A Cartoon History* (Boston, 1956), pp. 83 ff.

32. Anon., *Autobiography of a Happy Woman*, pp. 27, 104.

33. Austin, *Earth Horizon*, p. 162.

34. Gilman, *The Home*, p. 10 and *passim*.

35. Elizabeth C. Stanton, Susan B. Anthony, and Matilda J. Gage, eds., *History of Woman Suffrage*, I (New York, 1881), 70.

36. Anon., *Autobiography of a Happy Woman*, p. 5.

37. U.S. Commissioner of Labor, *Eleventh Annual Report*, p. 30.

38. *Report on Manufactures*, in Henry Cabot Lodge, ed., *The Works of Alexander Hamilton* (New York, 1904), IV, 91.

39. Abbott, *Women in Industry*, pp. 57–58.

40. N.C. Bureau of Labor Statistics, *Fifth Annual Report*, p. 296.

41. See Mary R. Beard, *Woman as Force in History* (New York, 1946).

42. Kate Hevner Mueller, *Educating Women for a Changing World* (Minneapolis, 1954), p. 237.

43. "The Fortune Survey: Women in America," *Fortune*, Aug., 1946, pp. 5–14; Sept., 1946, pp. 5–6.

44. Louis William Norris, "How to Educate a Woman," *The Saturday Review*, Nov. 27, 1954, pp. 9–10, 38–40.

45. Margaret Mead, *Male and Female* (New York, 1949), p. 382 and Chs. I and XVIII, *passim*.

46. Frances Corey, senior vice-president, R. H. Macy and Co., quoted in Katharine Hamill, "Women as Bosses," *Fortune*, June, 1956, p. 107.

47. Nassau County, N.Y., Vocational Education and Extension Board, *Nassau County Needs Vocational Education Now!* (Dec., 1955), II, 71.

48. See, for instance, Helene Deutsch, *The Psychology of Women* (New York, 1944); Ferdinand Lundberg and Marynia

Farnham, *Modern Woman: The Lost Sex* (New York and London, 1947).

49. See National Manpower Council, *Work in the Lives of Married Women* for discussion of many of these issues.

50. Abram Kardiner, *Sex and Morality* (New York, 1954), p. 224.

51. See National Manpower Council, *Womanpower*, Ch. VIII, "The Labor Market Behavior of Women."

52. Alva Myrdal and Viola Klein, *Women's Two Roles* (London, 1956), p. 183.

Index